WHEN YOUR ANIMAL DIES

WHEN YOUR ANIMAL DIES

by

SYLVIA BARBANELL

Foreword by
L. LIND-AF-HAGEBY
PRESIDENT LONDON SPIRITUALIST ALLIANCE
FOUNDER AND PRESIDENT ANIMAL DEFENCE SOCIETY

Spiritualist Truth Foundation

First published 1940
Reprinted 1944, 1946, 1950, 1955, 1961, 1969, 1979, 1987, 1995
This impression 2006

ISBN 978 0 85384 111 1

Printed in England by Booksprint

ACKNOWLEDGMENTS

The author desires to offer sincere thanks to the following bodies who have rendered assistance in supplying valuable data:

The Animal Defence Society
The Cats' Protection League
The International Institute for Psychic Investigation
The National Society for the Abolition of Cruel Sports

CONTENTS

FOREWORD
BY L. LIND-AF-HAGEBY

THE big St. Bernard dog lay dying. Panting, drawing with difficulty the last breaths. For twelve years he had been a wonderful friend, intelligent beyond description, loving, faithful, wilful, independent, troublesome. A character and an individuality of outstanding qualities.

As death drew quite close, he raised himself from his blankets on the floor with a supreme effort and, putting his head close to mine, looked into my eyes steadily, with deep and clamorous affection. The eyes said better than any words: "I am dying, but I shall live and be with you again."

The life of that dog had been to me a constant revelation' of "soul," a spur to further activities on behalf of suffering and ill-understood animals. The message in the eyes as he passed out of physical existence was a clear call to remembrance of the immortality of his devotion.

This happened many years ago.

Some years later Barry—that is his name—came back in tangible and audible form, but I shall not tell that tale, for Mrs. Barbanell offers in this unique book an array of evidence of the survival of animals which will startle the sceptics and disconcert the orthodox.

She has written a book which is unique in its combined appeal to the humanitarian and the Spiritualist. The two categories of workers for greater comprehension of the ultimate purposes of human life are in reality one.

The subject of the book is not new. The novelty is the great volume of evidence of animal survival presented in clear, simple, common-sense language, the many and varied instances of the return and the presence of "dead" animals, the gathering of comfort for those who mourn their friends.

On the subject of the survival of animals it is interesting to note that the great religions and literature contain innumerable references, direct and indirect, uttered and implied, to this important question. The poets are mostly vague. They have praised in exquisite language the marvellous qualities of the dog, expressed the belief that such virtue and beauty of soul cannot die, their grief at parting, their hope of reunion. Byron's epitaph on a Newfoundland dog

> *But the poor dog, in life the firmest friend,*
> *The first to welcome, foremost to defend,*
> *Whose honest heart is still his master's own,*
> *Who labours, fights, lives, breathes for him alone,*
> *Unhonoured falls, unnoticed all his worth,*
> *Denied in heaven the soul he held on earth*

is, perhaps, the most explicit protest against the theological barrier. Wordsworth, Walter Scott, Lamartine, Robert Browning, Elizabeth Barrett Browning, and Matthew Arnold—to mention only a few—have written stirring poems on dogs. Mrs. Browning's tribute to her dog, Flush

> *With my hand upon his head*
> *Is my benediction said*
> *Therefore and for ever*

by the words "for ever" suggests immortality. But Robert Southey in his "On the Death of a Favourite Old Spaniel" has the courage to write without reserve

> *And He who gave thee being did not frame*
> *The mystery of life to be the sport*
> *Of merciless Man. There is another world*
> *For all that live and move... a better one!*
> *Where the proud bipeds who would fain confine*
> *Infinite goodness to the little bounds*
> *Of their own charity, may envy thee.*

And John Galsworthy wrote in *The Inn of Tranquility* (I should like to find that Inn): "If *we* have spirits that persist, they have; if *we* know after our departure who we were, they do."

In 1937 there was published a book entitled *Animals and a Future Life*, by the Rev. W. H. Cock, B.Sc., Director of Religious Education for the Diocese of York. A priest of the Church of England with a scientific bent of mind, Mr. Cock proclaimed his belief that if there is a future life for Man, a believer in the concept of evolution must claim a future life for every member of the animal kingdom, however lowly. Mr. Cock wrote that the Creator has not only evolved the genus *homo*. "He has too, evolved and is evolving on earth other genera which are also spiritual creatures, not necessarily inferior, ultimately, to Man, and who also have a hereafter for the further development of personality and character."

The author lays stress on the fact that *the organic world is one whole* and that nothing is completely isolated from the rest. This refreshing acknowledgment of a paramount truth should be a subject for meditation on the part of the many exponents of religion who treat animals as if they were things, or mistakes of the Creator, or just temporarily animated depositories for beef and bacon.

There is no getting away from the fact that we are, by the laws of evolution and organic life, closely associated with the animals. Mrs. Barbanell draws attention to the embryological ties. The line of complete division, of absolute demarcation, is simply nonexistent. I was talking the other day to a man, highly versed in what he conceived to be the tenets of the Protestant Christian creed, who assured me that Man is completely separate from the lower creatures. "Don't you think there is a queer mix-up?" I said.

"Certainly not," he replied.

"Well, you need only read your Bible to find that Adam and Eve were in the midst of a zoological show, that, when Noah was told to enter the Ark for safety and perpetuation, he had to take an imposing crowd of non-humans with him, that Christ was born in a stable, that…"

He interrupted me by saying that did not show that animals were of any spiritual importance. I interrupted him by solemnly declaiming: "For the very creatures shall be delivered from the bondage of corruption into the glorious liberty of the sons of God. For we know that every creature groaneth with us also and travaileth in pain even unto this time." I was on the point of going on to the most significant and illuminating tale of Balaam's ass, when my friend fled!

Students of comparative religion have given inadequate attention to the great part which the animals play in the religious systems of the world. They have certainly failed to extract the humanitarian implications. The totems of primitive races, the wide-spread acceptance of the belief in human reincarnation in the forms of animals, the worship of animals, and the setting aside of certain species as sacred and protective to humanity are of a significance which transcends the merely curious.

In ancient Egypt many animals were sacred, invested with divinity, incarnations of gods. The dog was an important personage, the cat the object of a soul-searching cult. In the Bulletin of the Museum of Fine Arts of Boston, Dr. George Reisner, a well-known archæologist, some years ago told the story of an Egyptian dog buried with great pomp and ceremony. The stone inscription relating to the burial of this dog, who by order of the King (2,600-2,450 B.C.), was given a fine tomb, shows that the dog was called the "Bodyguard of His Majesty," and so distinguished that he might enter the after-life as an honoured spirit before the Great God. The intention was to assure the attendance of the spirit of the dog on the spirit of the King.

The souls of animals, the inter-relation of spirit-incarnation in men and animals, the links of charity and affection, the obligations of kinship are set forth in Hindu and Buddhist scriptures, in the religious teachings of ancient Persia and China, in Greek and Scandinavian mythology, in the famous humane Edicts of Asoka, Emperor of India. And do not let us forget the stories of the Christian saints: St. Francis preaching to the birds and exhorting the wolf to be good (why should he if they have no souls?), St. Roch served in time of distress by his dog, St. Jerome and his lion, St. Columba and the crane, St. Cuthbert and the otters, St. Bernard and the hare.

The great outstanding characteristic of the saints of Christendom is their pity for animals, their choice of them as companions and helpers, and their sense of unity with the inferior creatures of God. It is strange that many of those who now pray to these saints (a form of Spiritualism not generally recognised as such) should despise the beasts. When great nations seek symbols and emblems of power they find them in the mental strength and qualities of such animals as the lion, the eagle, the bear, the cock. The contempt of animals (which is a source of cruelty) is decidedly lop-sided.

A life of much reading has led me to put books in two classes: the vital and the manufactured. The vital books are the direct outcome of living intensely, of observation and search for truth, of the full mind and the generous heart. There are others which are just essays in words, repetitive of the thought of others, clothed sometimes in the froth and foam of the literary jargon of the day, or in the current psycho-analytical solvents of human perplexities. The difference can also be stated in the terms of sunshine and moonshine.

Mrs. Barbanell's book is of the variety which may be called vital. It is lively, entertaining, suggestive, provocative; it deals with matters which to the ignorant are impossible ("impossible" were at times all the discoveries and inventions of our modern civilisation, the use of steam as a propelling power, telephone, telegraph; flying, wireless telephony). It deals with incredible happenings in the seance-room, with evidence of the survival of men and animals, observed, noted, collected and told by the author. It touches wide issues: the postmortem conditions of fellow creatures on this planet whom we conveniently call "animals," and the ultimate consequences of the biological relationship between human beings and the creatures which appear in fur and feather.

The book should be read by Spiritualists. It should be read: by opponents of Spiritualism, by those of the superior and fully-fashioned mind who are sure that acceptance of the evidence of survival is the result of credulity, hallucination, or cleverly designed fraud.

Spiritualism today in English-speaking countries is a movement of immense proportions, a faith and a practice which guide the minds of millions. It is not a religion, but the fount and basis of all religions. The Christian, the Jew, the Mohammedan, the Hindu in search of origins and fundamentals all meet in Spiritualism, i.e., the recognition of the facts and actuality, historic and present, of inspiration, vision, of super-sensual sight and hearing.

The story of the efforts of the human mind to find reality presents few more outstanding examples of the lack of logic and consistency than the treatment of the evidence of survival provided by Spiritualism. Survival is the hope and the theme of all religious observances, of the churches, the chapels, the temples. It is the cardinal interest and the beautiful dream of art, of poetry, music and architecture. *Remove the hope of survival from the literature of the world and the foundations fall.* Yet those who bring the *evidence,* the knowledge which should take the place of faith and hope have been treated as mental defectives or as dangerous impostors.

It cannot be said too often that the nature of the evidence presented—now recorded in a vast armoury of literature—is as good, nay, better than, that generally accepted as accurate and reliable. Take a highly respectable tradition-hallowed court of law. Witnesses are heard, their testimony is accepted on the assumption that they can see, hear and remember accurately. Judgments are delivered on such testimony. Take a laboratory where physical and chemical questions are studied and theories formulated on the basis of the testimony of research workers who use their senses and their mental faculties of judgment. The evidence of Spiritualists is based on analogous experiences of sight and hearing, of close and careful observation and, in the scientific aspects of psychic investigation, on the use of apparatus, photography, and stringent conditions of control.

I have written of the nature and credibility of Spiritualistic evidence of survival. Such a reminder is not needed by those who have knowledge and experience. But those who have none will probably charge the author of this book with making assertions unsupported by critical examination of conditions under which the phenomena took place.

Mrs. Barbanell states that it is outside the province of her book to enumerate the wealth of evidence demonstrating man's survival. There are dozens of books, she reminds her readers, filled with incontestable proofs. The principal object of the book is to demonstrate that there is an impressive accumulation of evidence showing that it is not only men, women and children who survive the change called death, but also animals. The impelling motive is to give solace and certainty to the many who mourn' their animal friends.

The implications are far-reaching. If animals survive, if they, too, pass their physical lives in preparation for a progressive hereafter, there are uncomfortable conclusions to be drawn,, uncomfortable for those who merely exploit them, who believe that they were created solely for the "use" of men, uncomfortable for those who slaughter, chase, trap, imprison and torture them. Supposing we meet again? Supposing animals are not *things* 'which we can use as we please, soulless material for irresponsible sport or "scientific" mutilation? The dignity and superiority of Man are in jeopardy.

In "The Universal Kinship" Howard Moore wrote of Man: "In origin, disposition and form he is no more divine than the dog who laps his sores ... or the unfastidious worm who dines on the dust of his feet. Man is not the pedestalled individual pictured by his imagination—a being glittering with prerogatives and towering apart from and above all other beings." Darwin startled his contemporaries by writing that he would as soon be descended from that heroic little monkey who braved his dreaded enemy to save the life of his keeper... as from various still extant races of mankind.

The recognition of mind in animals and the fact: that there is no absolute line of demarcation between the mental processes of animals and men has become the foundation of current humanitarianism. We call not only for pity for the "lower" animals, but for understanding and justice. We know that all the precious qualities of soul which are the objects of moral and religious exhortation are not limited to the human form. Animals show love, devotion, faithfulness, comradeship, self-sacrifice, bravery, endurance in high degree. The degree and quality of intellect varies in them as in men. They are individuals addicted to personal likes and dislikes, prejudice and judgment, like human beings. Their human detractors seek escape from the logical consequences of acknowledging this truth by comparisons between the fly and the great musical genius. Why not compare the highly intelligent elephant with the congenital idiot?

Readers of Mrs. Barbanell's book will find ample food for thought in her references to the famous thinking, speaking, counting dogs, to the brave canine heroes of war, savers of human life. My own conversations with Kurwenal, Fips, Droujak, and other educated dogs have been of great psychological interest, to me a liberal education in the art of seeing ourselves as others see us. The thought of a dog's well-considered opinion of superior humans may be comical to the obtuse. It certainly is disconcerting to the self-exalted.

The idea of group-souls into which the spirits of animals sink at death and the belief that only our love endows them with powers of survival I cannot accept. The group-soul is no doubt a convenient term for the *herd-like behaviour of men and animals* in time of crises and fear. Psychic contagion, suggestive anger and propaganda may turn whole sections of humanity into one group-mind for the time being. But that does not permanently destroy individuality.

We are apt to recoil before the magnitude of the vision, in the words of Milton, of millions of creatures "walking the earth unseen both when we wake and when we sleep." It is more convenient to dissolve them into qualitative groups. But the close and patient student of individuality in the meanest creature that walks, flies and swims, of the wonders and mysteries of life is more cautious.

After all, we human beings in the grandeur of civilisation—a civilisation which at the present time is undergoing a severe test—will in all probability have to mount an evolutionary ladder which may in time and eternity move us as far above our present selves as we appear to be above the worm at our feet.

Let us be generous and appreciative of the worm.

INTRODUCTION

WHEN a dog belonging to some friends of mine passed over, I searched my mind as to what comfort I as a Spiritualist could offer these two people in the loss of their "only child."

For that is what Bill was to them. It is no use saying: "What nonsense! Much as one loves a dog, it cannot be the same as losing one's own flesh and blood, sad though it may be when a beloved pet passes on."

But I still emphasise that there are many cases when, to childless couples or lonely people in particular, an animal has taken the place of a child and the loss of the physical presence can be just as poignant.

And apart from these, there must be many thousands of people who, having loved their pets very dearly, wonder what has become of them after they have passed on, and whether they will ever see them, again.

I received a heart-broken letter from Bill's owners. He had been ill for some time. The veterinary surgeon finally told them that there was no hope of the dog ever regaining even a reasonable degree of health. He was too old. He advised them to have Bill put painlessly to sleep. After deep consideration my friends at last came to the conclusion that the kindest thing they could do for their pet was to take the vet's advice.

And so, wrapped in his master's old dressing-gown that Bill loved so much, their pet went to sleep!

Now I cannot pretend that Bill, having grown old and somewhat touchy in consequence, was always a popular dog with other people. Once or twice he had snapped at friends of the family. Hospitable Lola and George had been most embarrassed and apologetic on behalf of their naughty "child," but there had never been any ill feeling. Bill had character and a strong personality and his occassional lapses from good manners were readily overlooked, for it was realised that he was really becoming an old man in his dog life.

Perhaps not until the little body was laid to rest at the bottom of their lovely country garden did Lola and George actually realise how much they missed the third member of their household.

In their new loneliness they were almost inconsolable. A thousand questions tortured their minds. They wondered whether they had done the right thing in hastening Bill's passing.

Knowing that I was a Spiritualist they wrote and asked me, "Do you really believe that a dog survives death? It seems incredible to us that so much love and faithfulness could be suddenly snuffed out.

They wanted so much to believe that their dog had survived, but they also needed facts to convince them.

How could I best help these two people? They were not Spiritualists and had never studied the subject very deeply, although they were sympathetically inclined towards it.

My friend Lola is a journalist of some standing. George, her husband, is an actor with a successful stage and wireless career. They are intelligent, sophisticated people. I knew that sentimental platitudes would not help them.

Had Bill actually been a human, I could have put my hand on a hundred books that would have given them evidence and facts of survival.

I knew there was strong evidence as well as a logical case for the individual persistence of animals. But when I tried as a first step towards helping them to get a worthwhile book on the subject, I discovered it was not so easy.

Certainly I found one or two books on animal survival, but they were either non-evidential or hopelessly sentimental—valueless to those who demanded proofs.

Now I have attended many seances where "dead" animals have returned to their human friends to demonstrate the fact that they still lived. By varying methods they have been able to prove their continued existence to their owners.

I know through my own experience that there is a natural law which enables "dead" humans to return to their loved ones. It is the same law which operates in the case of "dead" animals coming back to their owners. For, with animals as with human beings love is stronger than death.

Even apart from the evidence, there is a logical case that, since human beings survive "death," so also do their lesser brethren, the domesticated animals, who by their contact with us have developed individual personalities of their own.

Because the story of Bill is so typical of many a beloved animal, I quote extracts from the letter Lola wrote me soon after this dog passed on:

"We were greatly touched by your thought of Bill. I do pray that his little soul is happy somewhere and that we shall be with him again some day. I don't have to tell you how we still feel about him. Just writing this has brought the ache back into my throat. I've ordered a little marble stone for his grave and we haven't had the courage yet to go and fetch it—George and I are always hiding things from each other that might hurt. It's just a pain, but it will grow less… it must.

"The story about Bill goes like this:

"About twelve years ago, before we were married, George called at a police station to inquire about something he had lost. He saw a little fox terrier bitch being led away on a piece of string by policeman. George was told she had been there a week and 'her time was up'. The little dog looked back. It was more than George could bear. He asked if he could have her and took her home.

"Within a fortnight she presented him—much to his amazement —with five little fox-terrier puppies exactly like herself. One day, when they were still creeping about on their tummies, with their eyes closed, the mother ran out of the flat and was run over. George thinks the poor little soul was trying to get back to her rightful owners to give them her good news. Anyhow, he was left with five motherless babies.

"He fed them with Lactol administered with a fountain pen filler, but they began to get very distended tummies and he found it was

necessary to put melted brown sugar into their milk to help the
machinery to work.

"He fed the five little mouths every two hours, waking up in the
night, using an alarm clock, until they were sturdy little puppies,
able to lap up their own food. He found homes for them all—two
bitches and the other two dogs, and Bill was the pick of the litter.

"For the whole of his life he and George were inseparable
companions. Often when I used to see them going out for walks
together I would think how odd it would be to see the one going for
a walk without the other.

"Bill was *more* than a dog. He not only read our thoughts but
he anticipated them. He knew if one of us was going away. For
a day beforehand he would sit and tremble with his ears back in
anticipation of his loneliness. He had a sort of code by which he
anticipated our actions. If one brought out a book of stamps he
would be ready, waiting at the door, to go to the post. The sight
of a dinner jacket and boiled shirt spread out on the bed would
send him trembling with misery under the bed because it meant a
night of 'left alone.' Once when George was appearing in a play at
Eastbourne, I took Bill down for the week-end. We went from the
station to the hotel, and I arranged to take Bill round to George's
dressing-room during the matinee. Believe it or not, that dog *led the
way* from the hotel to Devonshire Park Theatre, round to the stage
door and right up to George's dressing-room—so infallible was his
black nose!

"What a lovely idea of yours to write that book! I'm sure it is
needed. I'm always meeting people who have lost a dog friend and
their grief is terrible. It would be a tremendous comfort to them to
know that the little soul travels on and that the small grave isn't the
end."

There are many people in a similar position to my friends who
having lost a dear friend in the animal world want to know whether
it still exists.

I hope this book will answer the many questions that arise through
perplexity and doubt and bring comfort to those who mourn for
their pets.

CHAPTER I

THE CASE FOR SURVIVAL

MAN survives death; he also retains his individuality, consciousness, character and memory.

This has been proved up to the hilt. It has been attested by men of such high scientific standing as Sir Oliver Lodge, Sir William Crookes, Dr. Alfred Russel Wallace, and other people of unimpeachable integrity in all ranks of life.

It is outside my province to enumerate the wealth of evidence demonstrating man's survival. There are dozens of volumes filled with incontestable proofs. My purpose is to deal with its implications. Since human beings survive, so, for the same reasons, must animals live after death. For over twenty years I have attended hundreds of seances. Again and again I have communicated with the so-called dead who, to my complete satisfaction, have proved their continued existence.

It is impossible for a séance to take place without the presence of a human medium—that is, a person who possesses psychic gifts. But whether we are aware of it or not, most of us have a certain amount of mediumistic power, which can be increased and developed in our own homes. Thousands of ordinary people hold regular séances, or home circles, as they are called, in order to stimulate their latent psychic faculties. Many well-known mediums have discovered their gifts in this way.

Mediums can be compared with wireless receivers. Our ears, because their range of hearing is limited, are unable to register the delicate sound waves that are caught by wireless sets. Mediums, because they are sensitive, are able to tune in to a range of subtle vibrations that are lost to our normal hearing.

I have heard newcomers to Spiritualism say, "Why should I have to use a medium if I want to talk to my 'dead' husband? Why can't he talk to me direct?"

The answer is that if one's husband were in another country he would still have to use a medium—though not a human one—if he wanted to communicate. He would use as his medium a telephone, telegraph, radio or whatever means were available.

This analogy applies to those who have passed to another sphere of existence. If they want to communicate with us, they must have channels for their messages. Mediums are the human instruments necessary for this purpose.

I have attended scores of seances where I have heard the living and the "dead" carry on ordinary every-day conversations.

I have also been present at the most touching and moving re-unions between the "dead" and the ones left behind who are still linked to them by bonds of love and friendship.

Some spirit communicators whom I have heard were, when on earth, of exalted rank. Some who have proved their survival were scientists, theologians, cultured and erudite men and women. I have heard the voices of "dead" men whose names remain household words although they themselves have left the world which they enriched with their knowledge.

In contrast with the famous ones who have returned from Beyond, I have witnessed moving reunions between the most humble and ordinary men and women and their loved ones. Perhaps these have been the most poignant of all.

The seance room becomes Life's theatre, where tragedy and joy, humour and pathos, all mingle and play their parts.

Through mediumship I have witnessed many "miracles" which were merely the manifestations of supernormal, yet natural laws.

I have seen and spoken with my brother since his passing. His "solid" form took shape before my eyes. He made himself visible by using a substance known as ectoplasm, a kind of white vapourish stuff which exudes from some mediums at seances. It is partly physical and partly ethereal. Ectoplasm is visible. It has also been handled by many scientists.

This substance is used by the "dead" when they wish to build a reproduction of their earthly bodies for the purpose of recognition.

These forms do not necessarily look like the conventional, ghosts of popular fiction. They seem as solid as you and I, with ordinary flesh-and-blood features.

This form of mediumship is known as materialisation. When my brother, who passed over in the Great War, appeared at one of these séances, he called me by name and then took my hand in his own. It was not the cold, clammy hand of the traditional ghost. It was warm and human.

My brother solved, with a few short sentences, a fifteen year old mystery concerning his passing. It was a problem that had completely puzzled all his family because of the contradictory statements made at the time of his "death."

My parents had an official communication from the War Office saying that their son was "Missing, believed killed" on a certain date.

To our great joy, however, a friend of his received a letter from him dated a few days after the one on which he was reported "Missing, believed killed." There was no address in my brother's letter, but it was posted from a town in the war area in France. In this communication he said he was in hospital, wounded, but did not want his parents to know he had been injured.

But our renewed hopes gradually began to diminish as time passed and nothing more was heard from him. Correspondence between my parents and the War Office complicated matters still further. When they were put in touch with the officer who censored my brother's letter, he confessed that he was completely puzzled.There was no hospital of any kind in the town from which the letter had been posted! Neither had any men from his regiment ever been there.

Here was an insoluble mystery. Eventually we were forced to conclude he had passed over. But in what circumstances we could not tell.

This confusion was, however, ended when my brother spoke at the séance. He told me he was badly wounded and taken prisoner by the Germans on the date he was reported "Missing, believed killed."

He did not want to upset my parents with these tidings. He therefore wrote to a great friend and gave the letter to another English prisoner who had made plans to escape. This soldier succeeded in getting safely away and reached a town in France. Here he posted the letter.

The censor had, apparently, failed to notice that the letter could not have been written in the locality from which it was posted. Hence his perplexity when my parents afterwards got into touch with him.

My brother went on to tell me that he "died" of his wounds soon after his comrade escaped. Not only was his explanation of all that had happened lucid and reasonable but his conversation showed that he had a perfect knowledge of all that had perplexed us about his passing.

During this séance, he gave me further proof of his identity. He asked for a pencil and paper, and then his materialised hand wrote me a short letter.

I have since compared this writing with several letters he sent my mother from the Front. The writing is identical—even to the same manner of finishing his letters and the same way of signing his name.

I can vouch for the fact that the medium, Mrs. Helen Duncan, had never seen his earthly handwriting, and at the time of the séance I did not have in my possession any of his letters.

You may perhaps exclaim, "What nonsense! I have never heard such fantastic claims. I don't believe it."

Nevertheless, it is true.

Evidence of survival is available to most of us who seek for the truth in earnest sincerity, and with minds unhampered by prejudice and creed-bound superstitions.

Since the physicists' revolutionary discovery that the atom could be split, science has, in recent years, been forced to abandon many of its claims as to the indestructibility of matter. There is, today, no scientist of repute who would deny that matter, as a solid substance, is a kind of illusion. The physicists have demonstrated, that matter really consists of a collection of particles charged with electricity.

Our physical make-up must therefore be considered in terms of electronic radiations. Our apparently solid bodies, as well as the seemingly solid furniture we use in everyday life, can be disintegrated and transformed into non-material substances.

The death-blow to materialism has been dealt by the physicist. And, difficult though it sometimes may be to discard the patient investigation of years, the honest scientist must follow truth wherever it may lead.

Matter is indestructible. Though a piece of paper can be burned, it cannot be destroyed. Only the form is changed. Even the ashes may be resolved into chemicals. One cannot make something into nothing. It is true to say that matter is eternal.

Again, the secret of life cannot be explained in material terms. No one has succeeded in creating life, in making something from nothing. Life can be reproduced, but it cannot be created.

As matter is indestructible, it is logical to assume that life, too, is indestructible. There is no reason why life should cease merely because its material instrument has ceased to function.

Actually, "death" is due to the fact that life has withdrawn. It now functions on another plane of existence. This is proved by the fact that, again and again, those who have passed on have returned to prove that "death" has not robbed them; of their individuality.

The eminent scientist, Sir Oliver Lodge, once declared, "My hypothesis is that they [the 'dead'] are all round about us, in what we call the ether of space rather than in matter; that intercommunion is still possible...

"It is well to remember that we are immortal spirits in temporary association with matter. Probably it is through this bodily restriction and isolation that we become individualised and acquire a permanent personality, which hereafter is able to adapt itself to new surroundings, in accordance with the well-studied biological adaptability of the rest of animate existence."

What part of the individual returns from the other side of the grave to demonstrate and prove this greatest of all truths? Spiritualists know that it is the indestructible spirit, the real ego, whose cast-off physical body is no longer needed in a new phase of existence.

The individual who once functioned through the now discarded mass of radiation—the body—is the self-same person after he or she has passed over. "Death" has changed neither the character nor the real personality.

This fact is demonstrated in seance rooms all over the world. The "dead" constantly return to prove that they are the same ones we knew and loved before they passed into a larger and fuller life.

Human beings, in common with their lesser brethren, belong to the animal kingdom. They have a common ancestry. Although they have progressed along different lines, the same tree of evolution has borne their separate branches. Where, then, lies the discrepancy wide enough to suggest that, while one branch of the tree survives "death," the other branch, sprung from the same root, perishes?

Ignoring, at this stage, all the psychic evidence which supports the facts of animal survival, let us examine the case in the light of reason alone. First, take the purely physical aspect. It is known that the cells of the human body are no different in composition from those that make up the body of an animal.

Our skeletons, too, are composed of the same substance as the animals. We also breathe and expire in the same manner. The anatomy of the human being is comparable with that of other vertebrates in the animal kingdom.

Before the birth of each one of us, the wonderful story of evolution is re-told within the span of a few short months. What amazing changes take place in the growing embryo which develops in turn fish, amphibian and reptilian phases! In its lower mammalian stage, the human embryo even has a tail.

It is indeed a strong evolutionary link that binds us to our animal friends.

But let us even disregard this physical bond and see where we are when we examine the mental attributes of the human being and the domesticated or higher animal.

Although no forms of animal, bird or insect life are excluded from a degree of survival, their continued existence is on a different plane for reasons that will be dealt with separately.

It is only through a process of many thousands of years that the human being has developed his higher attributes and faculties.

At some period in the history of human development, consciousness dawned and man became aware of himself. Perhaps it was at the stage where he awoke to his own great potentialities that man began to express himself as an individual with an individual spirit.

With the dawn of individual consciousness, his moral and mental qualities began to develop. It was the growth of these higher attributes which gave man his supremacy' in the animal kingdom.

But if man has progressed in a more specialised way in the path of evolution, it does not mean that the animals are entirely outside this mental zone. Because of their close association with human beings, domestic animals have acquired, or "caught," some of man's individuality, consciousness and personality.

Has not the dog developed such qualities as love, sympathy, trust and loyalty? He often exhibits high intelligence, and in addition to his animal instinct he has also developed reasoning power to a marked degree. The domestic animal can express such human qualities as pleasure and joy, as well as dislike and mistrust.

Generally speaking, only the domestic animals who have acquired "human" qualities through their contact with man return to demonstrate their individual survival of "death."

Untamed creatures, and animals, who have not lived amongst us as friends and pets, also survive "death," since the same natural law operates for all living things. But there is a difference in the quality of their survival. We are told by those who have communicated from Beyond that non-domestic animals survive as part of a "group" or "herd" soul of the species.

Perhaps the sub-men and early primitive races of mankind had an analogous or similar "mass" soul and that only with the dawn of consciousness did the human spirit separate from the mass soul of his species and begin to function as an independent spiritual being.

Mind, character and individuality are the human qualities that survive "death" and continue to find expression in another form of existence.

The higher animals have also acquired similar aspects of consciousness. They, too, continue to exist as individuals after their physical bodies, composed of cells like our own, have perished.

Often, as on earth, an animal has to seek the aid of a human before he can return to his earthly owners. As in the case of humans, love bridges the gap between the two worlds.

Many a sorrowing human heart has been comforted by the knowledge that the mourned animal friend still lives.

CHAPTER II

DOGS WHO THINK

THE same qualities in man that persist beyond the grave are possessed by the domestic animals. They, too, continue to express these non-physical attributes after the physical body has been cast off

Man has for centuries visualised God in his own image as a Deified Super-Man. The dog, in his humility, has made no other god than man! And almost any scruffy little mongrel would gladly give his life to serve the God-Man who pays his licence.

To be British is also to be a lover of dogs. It is part of our national character. The "Englishman's home" is not really typical without the dog member of the family who shares the household joys and sorrows as a matter of course.

Lord Northcliffe proved his knowledge of the British character by the success of his newspaper. When the "Weekly Dispatch," as it was then called, was losing circulation, its editor searched for a series that would stimulate its sales.

There was brought to him a script received in automatic writing through the mediumship of the Rev. G. Vale Owen, an Anglican clergyman, describing life after death. The editor showed the script to Lord Northcliffe, who, turning its pages, saw a chapter dealing with dogs in the next world. "Everybody's interested in dogs and what happens to them," said Lord Northcliffe, who gave instructions for the script to be featured and for it to be extensively advertised.

It raised the sale of the newspaper from 350,000 to just under a million!

There is little to be said about the character of the dog that is not

fully realised and appreciated by anyone who has associated with
him—and who hasn't? We all know that our own dog is *the* most
intelligent, most lovable animal in the world. We all know that our
own pet differs from all other dogs. He's got that little "something"
the others haven't got.

Exactly! For a dog's individuality is just as distinct from his next-
door neighbour's dog as one human's personality is from another.

I do not contend that even the most intelligent dog in the world
has the high mental ability, the imaginative perception, or the
inventiveness of man. Such a contention would be stupid and
neither increases nor lessens the case for the survival of animals.

A dog could not write an oratorio, or execute a work of art. A dog
could not manage a department store or become a stockbroker.

Neither could a dog cheat, lie, nor slander his neighbour.

The scope of an animal's mind has a different range from the
human one. But even within his more limited scale, he does not
descend to some of the pitiably mean tricks that the inventive brain
of man can devise. No dog has ever been born with the ability to
plunge continents into darkness and despair. Only the brain of man
has achieved such great ambition.

Yet the dog, in his own sphere, can attain heights similar to the
ones reached by lofty and noble human souls, Selfless love, service,
devotion to duty, courage, sacrifice, compassion-all these qualities
have been expressed time and again by the dog.

He has laid down his life for his friend—man—and "greater love
hath no dog than this…"

For thousands of years the dog has been closely associated with
human domestic life. He, possibly, more than any other animal, has
identified himself with us. The dog prefers human companionship
to that of his own species. Indeed, there must be good in mankind
to have been chosen as his friend.

Close association has forged a link of strong understanding
between the dog and the human which has developed a very high
standard of intelligence in the animal.

This high degree of mental ability has been encouraged and
trained by certain animal owners. There is testimony' available

regarding over sixty animals—including forty-four dogs—who have learned to speak their thoughts intelligently by means of an alphabetical code taught by their owners.

After they mastered the alphabet and learned to count, the dogs were able to convey their own thoughts either by tapping their paws, by barking, or by both methods. Thus they could converse and exchange points of view with their human friends.

The high intelligence displayed by many of these: animals has brought them fame. Their mental powers have been investigated, studied and written about by scientists, professors, savants and psychologists. These animals have been visited by scores of famous people from different parts of the world who have been deeply impressed by the amazing intelligence exhibited.

At the well-equipped headquarters of the Animal Defence Society can be found a wealth of fascinating literature and information about these "educated" animals. They have, proved beyond a shadow of doubt that they possess individual minds of their own, with definite likes and dislikes. They have proved that they have memory and powers of reflection. They have demonstrated qualities of humour, reason, and sometimes a certain psychic ability. In addition, some of these animals have solved problems of arithmetic that confounded many a human used to dealing with mathematics.

It was by accident that the owner of Rolph, the celebrated Airedale terrier of Mannheim, discovered the dog's aptitude for doing sums. Paula Moekel, the dog's owner, has put on record in "Muenchner Nachrichten," how when she punished her little daughter for inattention and lack of ability to do an easy sum in the school room, she saw Rolph gazing with very sad and expressive eyes at the chastised child, as though he wanted to help her.

"Seeing this," wrote Paula Moekel,. "I exclaimed: 'Just see what eyes Rolph is making! It looks as if *he* knew what you do not!' No sooner had I said this than Rolph, who had been lying under my writing table, got up and came to my side. In surprise I asked him: 'Well, Rolph, do you know what two plus two amounts to?'

Whereupon the animal tapped my arm with his paw *four times*— we were all speechless!"

With successful results, she questioned the dog that day on numerals up to a hundred. After that, he was taught sums in the same way as one would teach an intelligent child. His studies gave him pleasure.

At a later date his owner said to him, "If you could say yes and no, you would be able to talk to us; now, look here. When you want to say *yes,* give us your paw *twice,* and if *no* then give it *three times. "* She immediately put this suggestion to an easy test. "Would you like to be spanked?" she asked Rolph. He returned a decided no. Then when asked if he would like some cake, he replied promptly in the affirmative.

"At length his alphabet came into being," writes his owner, "he having, with the exception of one or two letters, put it together entirely by himself. I would ask him, for instance, 'Rolph, how many taps with your paw are you going to give me for *a*? He then gave me a number which I carefully noted down. To my inexpressible pleasure I found that Rolph never forgot the numbers he had given, though I, to this day, must have my notes to hand whenever Rolph wishes to tap out anything.

"It is also remarkable that on a nearer investigation of his 'alphabet' it becomes evident that the letters Rolph requires least are made up of the highest numbers, whereas those to which he has constant recourse have their equivalents among the lower numbers. What he raps out is, of course, phonetically spelt, just according to how it sounds to him, and we have not attempted to worry him with orthography. His own original remarks are delightful."

I have quoted the beginning of Rolph's education with some detail as an indication of how these "talking" dogs use their own initiative right from the beginning of the education in which they take such a great interest.

Lola, a clever offspring of Rolph's, could talk, tell the time, and often work out the answer to a sum that had been set her even before her human owner could supply it. Lola's gifts, which have received wide attention, have been attested by many reputable people.

The story of Lola has been written by her owner, Henny Kindermann, in the book bearing that title and has been translated into English by Agnes Blake.

Henny Kindermann acquired her when she was quite a puppy. She tells in her book how she encouraged and developed Lola's own individuality, and how she trained her to transcribe her thoughts into the paw-rapping language she had taught her.

Most dogs have a very good sense of time. After Lola had learnt to read the time according to the clock, she would invariably be able to indicate the right time, although away from the sight of any time-keeper.

Lola possessed the most lovable disposition, a grand sense of humour, and rather too great an affection for food. This love of her "tummy" manifested itself in most of Lola's conversations!

Once when her owner asked her why she talked so much about food, Lola answered, "I from my food derive too little nourishment."

Her own individuality was very pronounced. Henny Kindermann records the following dialogue between them:

"Lola, would you like to be a human being?" "No."

"Why not?" showing the dog a biscuit. Lola (promptly): "I eat."

"No, not till you have answered." "Because of work."

A little later Henny Kindermann said: "Do you belong to me, Lola?" Very energetically, "No."

"To whom do you belong then?" "To myself."

"And to whom do I belong? Do I belong to you?" "No."

Food, hunting and marriage were the dog's wishes for her father's birthday, writes Henny Kindermann, who considers the first one "the central idea in a dog's thoughts. Yet, how necessary are all these three wishes to the maintenance of species, urged ever onward by the driving power of hunger and of love. After all, there is something very simple and direct about an animal."

I do not profess to understand Lola's reply to her owner's question as to why dogs prefer human. company to that of other dogs.

Lola's answers implied that dogs had in some past epoch made an oath or promise to each other concerning humans.

Further questions as to why this promise had been made brought this reply, "Because of their [humans] eyes and their sorrows without ceasing."

Whether there is, or is not, any esoteric or inner significance about this "promise," I confess, I am entirely ignorant. But it is touching, nevertheless, even if it only arose in one dog's individual mind.

The dog's owner once asked, "Lola, what will become of you when you are dead? What will become of your body?" The dog replied that it would go to heaven. "And then," writes Henny Kindermann, "I asked, 'Do you know what a soul is? And she said, 'Yes.'

"'Have I a soul? 'Yes.'

"'Has a stone one? 'No.'

"'And a horse? 'Yes.'

"'And water? 'No.'

"'Have all dogs? 'Yes.'

"What do dogs feel when they look at the eyes and see the sorrows of people?" the author asked Lola, who replied that dogs felt love. "To this day I feel touched at these answers," Henny Kindermann writes.

"How often in trouble and in sorrow," she continues, "have we not found relief in a dog's sympathy and been glad to call it a friend in our sufferings? How often has not a dog's eyes filled with understanding when its master has sat alone and lost in grief, coming, perhaps, and gently laying its head upon his knees, fixing its faithful gaze on him until at length he might be moved to smile, feeling that, after all, he was not alone? Dogs! May this not be your true vocation?"

The most celebrated educated dog was Kurwenal, of Weimar, who has now passed on. This famous dachshund was fortunate enough to be owned by one of the leading figures in the animal protection movement, one who has devoted herself to the task of proving that animals have a mental and soul life.

Mathilde, Baroness von Freytag-Loringhoven, a woman of out-standing intellect, with a distinguished artistic career, was born in

Copenhagen, and later took up residence in Weimar. It is due to her understanding of animals that Kurwenal learned to express himself with such astoundingly successful results.

Kurwenal was taught to speak in a language of barks. Not only could this thinking, counting, reading dog answer questions intelligently, but he would offer his own opinions and make independent observations on men and affairs of the world.

In one year alone seventy-four experiments were made with Kurwenal by five hundred investigators.

To everyone who questioned him, either orally or by writing, he gave, without hesitation, different answers. He also took part in conversations without being asked.

He loved to display his knowledge and told his owner, "To me learning is a great happiness." In fact, the Baroness once wrote, "At every hour of the day, Kurwenal was ready for his 'greatest happiness'—conversing with mankind."

A man was discussing with the Baroness the lack of understanding of dogs held by some people. "They judge without knowing anything about the true nature of dogs," he said. Kurwenal broke into the conversation at this point, with a spontaneous, "I have often experienced this."

During the visit of a young scientist, the dachshund told him, "I like to have you here. You are more sincere than most people."

On another occasion, Kurwenal gave a short resume of a three act drama the Baroness had written. He proved that he remembered the play which she had read aloud to her sister three years previously!

Kurwenal had a great affection for a certain general who used to visit him. The dog would talk to him alone, in the absence of his owner.

"The dogs generally do this," writes the Baroness in "Progress Today," the journal of the Animal Defence Society, *"contrary to the erroneous assertion that they only work when their teacher is present. They work with anyone they are fond of, and when they feel they are believed in and trusted."*

Kurwenal had a roguish sense of fun. The Baroness was given a very fine Roman rug for him on her birthday. Kurwenal said, "I find rug nice, will tear." Then he paused before he added, with a sly look in his eyes, "Not!"

Sometimes the dog would adopt a rather "cheeky" manner with learned men. A young neurologist and animal psychologist at the University at Berne wanted to test him. Kurwenal, who thought he had been investigated quite enough for that day, exclaimed, "I answer no doubters. Bother the asses."

The investigator laughingly replied, "But I believe in you. That is why I took the trouble to come here."

After that, the dog and the man talked together for nearly an hour. When the scientist was about to leave, he turned to the dachshund and said, "I nearly forgot to ask you what you think about a dog's soul.

"It is eternal like the soul of man," replied Kurwenal.

The Baroness says that the dog would sometimes speak of religious matters and would question her about all kinds of things. On one of these occasions he said to her, "I often pray." She asked, "What do you pray for?" Kurwenal answered, "For you."

The dog delighted in listening to explanations of things he did not know. Sometimes he would interrupt with, "This I have known for a long time," or "I have thought that before. Don't always tell me the same things over and over again!"

Professor Max Müller, a distinguished Continental veterinary surgeon, said of Kurwenal in "Progress Today:"

"This dachshund lives, in the intellectual sense, more in man's sphere than in the animal's."

He tells how the dog correctly named the kind and the number of flowers that the professor had brought with him to present to the Baroness Mathilde. The dog said that the roses "smelt lovely." He also correctly calculated some figures more quickly than his human investigator.

Kurwenal, who had learned about many famous men from his owner, could name the authors of certain quotations that had been previously read to him.

For instance, when the professor asked who wrote, "To be, or not to be," the dog replied, "Shakespeare."

Professor Max Müller says, "Kurwenal has an unusual thirst for knowledge, is interested in everything that goes on about him and grasps the purport of conversations conducted between human beings, even in cases where one would be inclined to assume that the dog lacks the faculty to understand the subject discussed."

During tea he was discussing with his hostess the slaughter of dogs for food, a brutality not consistent, they agreed, with human culture and civilisation. He thought that the topic must be of particular interest to Kurwenal and asked the dog whether he had followed the conversation. "Yes," replied Kurwenal.

"Do you wish to say something about it?" "Yes," answered the dog, and barked out the following: "The Christian religion prohibits killing."

Kurwenal's attractive personality and grand sense of humour made him beloved by all who knew him.

"I do love you so!" he once spontaneously exclaimed in his bark language to a woman friend of his owner.

"Oh! Don't try to make me believe that," she answered. At which the dog replied, "I always speak the truth."

When the Baroness told Kurwenal that his human friends at the Animal Defence Society were moving their headquarters, from one part of London to another, she asked what message he would like to send them, as she was forwarding his picture. She explained that entering a new house was an event of importance to humans. Immediately the dog barked out, "No flowers, therefore I send my picture with very many congratulations—Kurwenal."

This remarkable dachshund sometimes composed little rhymes. The Baroness tells how she was visited by a friend, an army officer, who was very sad because his wife had recently passed on. Kurwenal said to his owner, "We must cheer him up. The dog approached the downcast man. "Do you want to say something to him?" asked the Baroness. "Yes," replied Kurwenal.

"You can make up such nice little poems now," she said. "Make one for him."

Without much delay, Kurwenal recited:

> "I love no one as much as you.
>   Love me too.
> I should like you with me every day.
>   Of happiness a ray."

Touched by the intelligent dog's sympathy, the depressed man's spirits brightened considerably.

Baroness Mathilde, who has taught several dogs in Weimar to speak, says, "All dogs who can talk are happy; but not all dogs are suited for it, because all dogs do not want to learn."

In "Progress Today" Professor Max Muller sums up in these words his experiences with educated dogs: "It was a very interesting experience for me, as a veterinary surgeon, to observe these dogs, to hear and see their bark-and-tap language, based on a number alphabet, and to converse personally with them.

"Although by association with my own dogs I had been aware for a long time of the *independent thinking* of dogs, the case of the animals in Weimar proved particularly striking... These dogs show us what a wrong attitude we have towards the educated animal, how much the animal understands us, and how very little, as a rule, we understand the animal.

"The number-speaking dogs confound the human conceit, which would deny to animals the faculty of thought. The fact, which becomes clear to us, that the dog thinks, ponders, reflects and constructs independently, draws conclusions, calculates more quickly than we do, and that, after successful instruction, he reads and is able to speak by means of a number-alphabet, is something little dreamt of in our knowledge and which we have now the opportunity to acknowledge...

"To anyone... who has the capacity to draw the only admissible conclusion from the resulting communication between man and animal, and animal and man, it will become clear *that between the activity of the human and animal brain, on which thinking capacity depends, there is no basic dissimilarity but only a difference of degree.*"

He draws the following conclusion: "The number-speaking dogs compel us to recognise that the active brain in the dog is a mental organ similar to the active brain of man, and that the animal's directing mind working through the cerebrum is capable also of the faculty of reflection and thought."

Once, when I was talking to a friend about some of these educated animals, she said, "But isn't it cruel to teach them to do tricks?"

I hope I have made it clear that there is not the slightest suggestion of cruelty involved in training animals to express themselves just as one trains and encourages children.

The instruction of these dogs has always been conducted only by those who have the greatest affection for them.

The fact that their education has been followed with sympathetic interest by leaders in animal reform movements is enough to refute the suggestion that cruelty is involved.

This cannot be said of some of the experiments carried out by Pavlov and others in order to observe how certain animals behave and react under physical and mental stress and stimulus. These experiments, in the name of "science," are in quite a different category.

An erroneous inference should not be drawn from the fact that certain dogs, responding to specialised education, have developed amazing mental ability. This does not mean that the domestic animal who has never received such a training has less natural intelligence than these "mental aristocrats of the canine world.

How many of us humans have potential gifts that, owing to circumstances, have never been fostered and developed?

The "dog-in-the-street," like the "man-in-the-street, does not always get the opportunity to attract the special attention meted out to the chosen few. Not every human can devote the time, even if he wished, to develop the potential gifts of his own pet.

There is no doubt that the average dog has a high degree of intelligence, and has similar reasoning powers to his educated relatives. Even though every dog cannot converse with us as successfully as the specially trained ones, he has proved his ability to think for himself and to act independently. There, is a place in the scheme of things for the ordinary dog, as there is for the ordinary man.

Abraham Lincoln said, "God must have loved the common people—He made so many of them." The same may be said of the common dog.

We are constantly hearing authentic stories about canine pets proving their mental alertness.

Captain D. G. Shaw, a Surrey veterinary surgeon, tells in "Soul Of Animals," a most interesting pamphlet issued by the Animal Defence Society, how an Airedale patient showed marked reasoning powers. Captain Shaw found Ruff waiting outside his surgery door one day, and naturally concluded that his owner had brought him as on previous occasions. But seeing no trace of Ruff's owner, or of the car in which they usually arrived, he thought Ruff must have strayed. He therefore telephoned to his owner's home. "I was informed," writes Captain Shaw, "that the dog was in his kennel and it was suggested that I had mistaken my visitor for Ruff" Indeed, he was told that Ruff had recently disturbed a hive of angry bees, and had beaten a hasty retreat to his own quarters. No, the canine visitor waiting outside his doorstep could not possibly be their Ruff!

But, all the same, it was! Unobserved by his owner, the Airedale had, of his own volition, left his home and journeyed to the veterinary surgeon.

Captain Shaw tells how the dog jumped on to his operating-table where, upon examination, he found that he had been stung by bees!

"It is manifest that this dog correctly reasoned that by calling on me he would receive relief from the irritation he was suffering," says the vet, *"and it should be added that normally he never visited the town.* In fact his visits to me for previous treatment had been by car, and that he should quickly cover the intervening distance by road, and so rapidly, was another proof of his intelligence."

You might say, "That's not necessarily mental ability, but instinct, to run to the one who previously alleviated his suffering."

Well, even if you wish to reason thus, it is no different front the "instinct" which leads a sick human to the medical practitioner's door-step!

There is no doubt that our canine friends "take in" far more of the human conversation around them than we imagine. It is only when they perform an independent act that we realise how closely they follow what takes place in the home.

A friend told me she was discussing with her husband an unexpectedly hurried professional appointment he was obliged to make. Michael, a close relative, had made plans to call and say goodbye before leaving for his holidays that morning. It was a great disappointment to her husband that the unexpected appointment would take him from home before the time arranged for the goodbye visit of his relative.

The dog sat quietly while they talked over the matter. Then he asked to be let out of the house. Some time later, Michael called, well before the time originally arranged, because, as he said, "I found Bill barking outside my front door and thought I had better bring him back at once." Michael lived some little distance away, in a road with scores of houses, all looking alike. The dog had only been there twice before in a car. But he had set off definitely with the purpose of bringing my friend's relative to the house to say goodbye.

This is an instance of reasoned action on the part of an ordinary dog who had not received any special training or "education." Obviously he was able to follow the purport of the conversation of his human friends, and to act upon his desire to help them.

Other friends of mine had a mongrel dog named Whiskey. There was little that this sagacious animal did not understand. They would, on most mornings, give Whiskey a slice of bread and butter for his breakfast. Sometimes, when he was loath to eat it, they would say to him, "If you don't eat it, we'll give it to the birds!" This always had the desired effect. He would finish his breakfast!

Their accustomed admonition had an amusing sequel one morning, when the bread and butter seemed even less attractive than usual. Hearing the usual observation, "If you don't eat it, we'll give it to the birds," the dog gingerly picked up the slice of bread and butter. Holding it between his bared teeth, so that he could not get even a taste of the despised morsel, Whiskey carried the bread down the garden path. At the bottom of the garden, where the birds always received their tit-bits, he laid his own offering on the grass, not, I am afraid, in a very generous spirit, but as though to say, "Well, let the confounded birds have it; I won't eat it, anyhow!"

A rather touching story of a dog's intelligence is told by Miss J. L. Stephen in "Souls Of Animals." Jane, a wire-haired terrier was always appealing to visitors at Hayling Island to throw a ball so that she could chase it. Miss Stephen's blind brother-in-law was spending his holiday with her. Several times Jane approached him, wondering, no doubt, why he did not throw the ball for her to catch.

One day the dog looked quite intently into the man's face for about two minutes. She had a questioning look in her eyes. Then she tapped his right foot gently three times, and stepped back, waiting.

"She was not disappointed," writes Miss Stephen. "He stooped and threw the ball. Jane had discovered his infirmity."

CHAPTER III

ANIMALS WHO REASON

THE size of the horse has prevented it from sharing with humans the intimacy of the home. Nevertheless this large animal has, through long association with us, acquired some "human" qualities, and has displayed, on occasions, intelligence and mental ability far beyond instinctive sagacity.

The famous Elberfeld horses were taught to spell by their owner, Karl Krall. They answered questions by a system of stamping their hoofs. They solved the most complicated mathematical problems, even to the extent of extracting square and cube roots!

A number of eminent scientists testified to the thinking ability they displayed. Amongst many other famous people, Maurice Maeterlink paid a visit to the Elberfeld stables. One of the horses' solved mathematical problems which Maeterlink himself could not answer.

The horse refused to give the square root of a certain chance number which was offered to him. It was afterwards discovered that the particular number did not possess one!

Because certain people thought that visual signals were used by the trainer when he questioned them, he educated a blind horse. The successful tests made with this animal confuted these suggestions.

The Shetland pony, Black Bear, a jet-black stallion, was owned and trained by Mr. Thomas Barrett, of New York.

Mr. Arthur Goadby, an American psychical researcher, writes of his experiences with this equine wonder. He says that soon after Black Bear came into Mr. Barrett's ownership he discovered that the animal possessed remarkably high intelligence, as well as memory and quick comprehension of the spoken word. His owner therefore proceeded to teach Black Bear the alphabet, the spelling of simple words and elementary arithmetic.

"But to his surprise," writes Mr. Arthur Goadby, "he discovered that Black Bear had no sooner learned the rudiments of these subjects than he seemed to develop an intuitive proficiency in them far surpassing that of his master."

Although Mr. Barrett, a former ranchman, was a most interesting man, he had little schooling in his youth. He had no pretence to learning and was often perplexed by the variety of information, mathematical skill and imaginative powers of the pony who so rapidly surpassed his own store of knowledge in many directions.

Mr. Goadby decided to investigate the claims made on the pony's behalf. Casual observers would often ascribe the animal's accomplishments to trickery on the part of his master. Because they were perplexed, they averred that the ex-ranchman was a genius, a professional showman, or a student of historic and classic lore.

Mr. Goadby, too, was in a perplexed state of mind before he began his investigations of the abilities of this wonder animal. He says, "After many experiments in the course of the year I have convinced myself, and proven to others, by tests… that Mr. Barrett does not either intentionally or subconsciously prompt the pony."

Mr. Goadby paid his first visit to the animal with Mr. Bligh Bond, another psychic investigator.

The system of language and numbers the owner had taught Black Bear to use so as to make himself understood was a simple one. The animal would stand facing two racks upon which were suspended several rows of leather tabs which bore metal letters and numbers. In replying to questions, Black Bear would choose the appropriate tabs from the racks.

Mr. Bligh Bond proceeded, on their first visit, to test the animal's mathematical knowledge. Black Bear's replies were brilliantly and sensationally accurate. It was evident to the two investigators that they were in the presence of an extraordinary phenomenon.

Mr. Bligh Bond drew a square on a blackboard, and then drew a line from corner to corner. The pony was asked to give the name of the line thus drawn. Expecting to receive the answer, "Diagonal," he was amazed to have the quaint but nevertheless correct definition from the horse as "the line of the hypotenuse."

The investigator then asked the animal the length of the diagonal when the sides of the square were five units in length. Thepony instantly replied, "Seven," but retreating, shook his head as if demurring at this result. He seemed to realise that the correct amount, being absurd, could not actually be measured. Nevertheless, seven is the nearest approximation in whole numbers.

Further mathematical problems were put to Black Bear, who correctly answered them. When there were no answers to fit certain problems the pony would indicate correctly that he realised the position.

"Throughout these proceedings," writes Mr. Goadby, "I had closely watched Mr. Barrett, endeavouring to detect any code . but I could detect no signalling whatever."

Feeling assured of this, and realising that the pony's abilities were beyond those of any ten-year-old, equine or human, however great a genius, he concluded that the animal's powers could be explained only upon supernormal grounds.

He therefore proceeded to test Black Bear to see whether he could detect any pyschic ability. He had some success.

"Can you see any colour around my head?" he asked. Immediately the pony nodded, approached him, and softly placed his nose against Mr. Goadby's forehead.

"What colour?" continued the questioner. The pony, replied, "Light." Still expecting Black Bear to name a colour, he asked, "Light what?" Much to his surprise, the animal spelled out, "Rays." He had rejected his questioner's suggestion as to colour and had given his own independent impression.

On being asked further questions, the pony said he could see others in the room in addition to the ordinary occupants. He named the number of extra men and women he could see. Unfortunately,

Black Bear was interrupted when lie was asked whether he could give the names of the people lie saw who were invisible to the other humans in the room. Later, when he was questioned further on the subject, he indicated that these extra people had now disappeared.

Sometimes, Black Bear responded to telepathy, but not always when special experiments for the purpose were made.

Once, he was asked who was President of the United States in 1861. Black Bear replied, "Lincoln." Asked where he was assassinated, he replied, "Washington." Moreover, he gave the name of the President's murderer as "Booth," and said that Booth afterwards broke his leg. "What was Booth's first name?" somebody asked the animal. "Wilkes," replied Black Bear.

"Now I doubt if these questions had ever been asked him before," says Mr. Arthur Goadby. "Black Bear does not frequent libraries nor read books. He never went to college nor had a private tutor and is only eleven years old and spends almost all of his life alone in his stall and only occasionally does he go forth to give entertainments, and when he does he is giving information not acquiring it.

He goes on to say, "In the above conversation the reply concerning Booth's first name was a curious one. In the histories Booth is always 'John Wilkes,' but to his friends he was known simply as 'Wilkes.' How came Black Bear to state it that way? If he had learned it from books, he would undoubtedly have given the full name.

The pony's ability to give the answers to sums of addition, after simply glancing at rows of figures, is considered by Mr. Goadby to be supernormal. He also points out that Black Bear's unexpected replies to questions showed independent thinking, and sometimes his knowledge of historical events certainly surpassed what had been taught him.

In the experiments made by Mr. Goadby, rigid precautions were taken to avoid the possibility of any conscious or unconscious signals or codes between the horse and his owner. The tests seemed to him "definitely to establish the fact of the pony's independence and to dispose of any charge as to prompting by Barrett."

He considers that Black Bear exhibits the intellect of a highly cultured human being, and adds, "His knowledge, tact, wit, courtesy, and poise even his occasional manifestations of boredom and indifference, or sophistication and dislike, are all distinctly human traits."

In summing up the results of his experiences, the investigator of this equine prodigy says, "One might well be justified in the conclusion that Black Bear is just a normal though very intelligent horse; but that there are certain modulations of his supernormal nature that enable him to enter into *rapport* with discarnate and therefore invisible human beings."

We know that mediums can tune in to sources of knowledge beyond their own normal range. My own opinion is that Black Bear displayed similar capabilities, and that he was, in fact, an equine medium.

In addition to the specially trained and educated horses, there are well attested instances—as in the case of dogs—of the independent thinking ability of our equine friends. The following instance which took place during the last war, was told by an army officer in "Animal's Friend."

"A curious thing happened the other night," he writes. "A wagon full of bombs was expected at our dump. Eventually it [the wagon] appeared coming along the road. My sergeant shouted out directions to the wagon: 'Turn to the right, now to the left, now stop,' all of which it did. When the man went up to it there was no driver—he had got off some way back when the wagon was shelled, and turned up later! The horses had carried out directions on their own."

Another instance of equine intelligence was recently told in the "Daily Herald." Mr. Frederick Ford, J.P., a Suffolk farmer, became suddenly ill whilst working with his two old farm horses in one of his fields. Taking the initiative, they carried him home unattended, after he collapsed on the back of one of them. The newspaper reporter says, "The horses brought him across fields, through the village street, along the main London road with its three lines of traffic, and then crossing the road, down the lane to Mr. Ford's farmhouse."

The mare, Spot, led the way, followed by Blossom, with the sick man on her back. The village, who saw the procession, did not realise that the magistrate was ill. Mrs. Ford told the newspaper representative that the magistrate's collapse was due to a bad heart attack. She said, "The two old mares, which we have had for a number of years, walked into their stable after my husband had been lifted from Blossom's back. There they waited patiently to be unharnessed. There is no doubt that my husband owes his life to them!"

The magistrate remembered nothing of his collapse, or how he reached his own home.

Even with non-domestic animals, it has been found that, when contact with humans has been established, intelligent observation develops and they acquire personalities of their own. Indicative of this fact is the amusing incident related by Mr. H. Richard Jones, the Governing Director of the Animals' Friends Society. Here is the story in Mr. Jones's own words:

"Many years ago I had the honour to serve in the good ship *Maharajah* when she was tender to the Indian Penal Settlement at Port Blair, Andaman Islands.

"The industry of the Settlement at that time was the export of the rare Padouk timber that abounds in the forests of the Islands. The convicts were actively engaged in the work of felling and clearing; and a large herd of trained elephants was also employed.

"On one occasion when we lay at anchor in Port Blair harbour our genial and popular skipper, Captain Ray White, decided to celebrate his birthday with a luncheon party, and on the eventful day the ship was dressed 'over all' with bunting from eight o'clock in the morning-the customary hour for hoisting flags.

"Early in the forenoon watch the following signal was received from the shore semaphore station:

" 'O.H.M.S. From Chief Commissioner, Port Blair, to Commanding Officer *Maharajah:* Please undress ship. *Our elephants, seeing your flags, think it's a public holiday and refuse to work.* '"

Individuality and consciousness are not confined to animals alone. Feathered pets also possess their share when they are made "one of the family." Although it is a matter for each of us to decide for ourselves whether it is right, or not, to keep birds in cages, there is no doubt that those born in captivity appear to be quite happy.

And what character some of these pets display! It often makes me gasp that so much personality can exude from such tiny bodies.

My friend Mr. Hannen Swaffer has a Norwich canary who possesses individuality to a marked degree. When Mr. Swaffer and his wife returned from a holiday with another canary they had bought in Morocco, Dickie, their English bird, very much resented the new intruder.

When the grand new cage was placed against the window opposite his own, he was most indignant and twisted and turned his tiny head as much as to say "Foreign riffraff." I'm afraid this little Norwich fellow is very insular, a veritable Colonel Blimp of a bird.

I don't know whether the Swaffers caught Dickie's scornful opinion of the foreigner, but anyway they named the new bird "Riff"! But Dickie didn't pine away with jealousy. He could take it! Nevertheless, he steadfastly refused to sing a note while the other bird was present. If you wanted to hear Dickie's glorious song, you had, first of all, to put his rival in another room.

Anyway, poor Riff, who alas, was no songster, did not live a very long time; so once again, Dickie is "Cock of the Walk." He continues to welcome the regular visitors to Mr. Swaffer's flat with a vocal greeting of recognition.

When Mr. Swaffer plays Patience, one of his favourite; games, he often puts Dickie's cage beside him on the table. The little canary will perk his head to one side and fix his bright eyes on the cards. Really, I would hardly be surprised if, some fine day, he pointed a claw at a card and said, "Look, Swaff, there's a move right under your nose—the black ten on the red Jack, don't you see?"

There are people who keep a cat merely as a convenience for catching mice! But anyone who treats a cat as a member of the family knows that this animal has intelligence and reasoning power.

Perhaps this self-controlled, independent creature is the most fascinating of all our domestic pets. The cat does not usually wear her heart on her sleeve—perhaps I should say on her paw—yet, though seldom as demonstrative as the dog, she is capable of deep affection.

There is a popular misconception that cats get attached to houses and not to people. This does not apply to most cats. Although there are cases where they have strayed back to familiar haunts, there is often a significant reason behind this, not unconnected with human relationship. Most cats settle down quite contentedly in their new homes when their owners have had to change their addresses.

A number of stories of the intelligent reasoning power of cats have been recorded.

In "Souls Of Animals," Miss Irene Caudwell tells how on two occasions a household was saved by a cat from the serious effects of bad gas escapes. The first time was when the animal cried outside a bedroom door until the sleeper awoke and discovered the escaping gas. On another occasion the cat had been shut up for the night in the kitchen. Nevertheless, the frantic mewing led to the discovery of the leakage of gas. "The same cat," concludes Miss Caudwell, "also came and gave us warning when my mother had been taken ill and, unknown to us, was in another part of the house unable to move."

Mr. W. Tombleson, of New South Wales, has recently given a remarkable story to the London "Evening Standard" about a cat's reasoning powers. He watched the cat chase a snake into a bush. After waiting unsuccessfully for it to reappear, the cat trotted home and later returned with one of her kittens which she placed near the bush. The cat then hid. The snake reappeared on the scene and made for the kitten. This was what the cat had waited for. She attacked and killed the enemy.

Almost beyond the normal realms of reasoning on the part of an animal is this instance related by a doctor in "The Cat," a journal published by the Cats' Protection League. He writes: "On returning for luncheon after my morning round of visiting patients, I found a cat sitting on my front door step, and when I opened the door the cat walked in mewing piteously."

Thinking it must be hungry, the doctor offered it some milk, which it refused, meanwhile continuing to cry in a distressed manner. He stooped down to caress the cat, and discovered that it had a lump, under the angle of the jaw, which proved to be a large abscess. He took the cat into the surgery, opened and dressed the wound. It kept quite still during this operation, and made no attempt to scratch.

"As soon as I lifted it down from the table, it rubbed itself against my leg, writes the doctor, "and going into the hall drank the milk. It then went out of the door, but returned the following morning at the same time, when I dressed the wound."

On three consecutive mornings, the animal reappeared for treatment until the wound was practically healed. After that, the doctor never saw the cat again.

"I wonder," he concludes, "how the cat knew I was a doctor and could help it."

In the "Daily Express" there appeared a story of a kitten's intelligence which possibly saved the life of a gardener.

Nurse Nichols was preparing breakfast for an invalid, when she heard tapping on the window pane. A kitten was trying, by, this means, to attract her attention. She followed the animal into the garden, where it led the way to a shed. Here, the nurse found the gardener suffering from a stroke. Normally, no one would have gone to the shed until evening, by which time it would probably have been too late to save the life of the stricken man.

A rather amusing story of an animal's alertness of mind is told in "The Cat."

A black cat wanted to cross a busy main road at the crossing signals. As the red light was showing, he sat on the kerb and waited until the green light appeared. Then, he calmly crossed. This incident was witnessed by a number of people.

The London "Star" recently printed an account of a cat, living at Nunhead, who used to pull the bell at St. Catherine's Church to summon the worshippers! His sense of rhythm was accidentally discovered by his owners when he started playing notes on the piano with his paws! Then, one day, he accompanied the verger, who lives in the same road, to church. The musical cat stood on his hind legs and started tugging the bell rope. Within a few weeks he learned to ring the bell by himself, and few people in the neighbourhood realised that a cat called them to church on Sundays.

CHAPTER IV

"GREATER LOVE HATH NO—"

D URING man's evolution through the ages, he has developed many noble qualities in his nature. Men have laid down their lives for altruistic principles. and exhibited great fortitude and courage in the face of death.

Nevertheless, self-sacrifice and bravery are not the prerogative of the human being. Animals have reached similar heights of courageous daring and have given their lives, when necessary, in the execution of duty.

Great and heroic services have been rendered by dogs in time of war. They have proved themselves intrepid fighters, and disciplined soldiers.

"La Croix du Midi" reported a number of stories of parts played by dogs in France during the Great War. These stories of the war dogs of France were afterwards translated and printed in a pamphlet called "Souls Of Animals."

"During the war," runs the translation, "the 'faithful friend of man' was indeed man's most trusted companion. He was by turns a vigilant sentinel, a rapid liaison agent, a keen nurse, an indefatigable revictualler, and a police agent naturally full of flair. When he was not officially mobilised, he was simply the mascot of the company, the section or the squad. He marched on the left of the unit, was present at reviews, messed with the soldiers, and on winter nights slept under running fire. This dog with the human eyes was the joy of his companions, whose many cavillings he bore without too much complaint.

"The real war dog belonging to the Army had a registration booklet, an identity disc, equipment and a gas mask. He followed a course of training in the rear, and on completion of this was detailed to unit.

"These war dogs were intrepid fighters. Their devotion often cost them their lives; and they often saved the lives of their friends, the poilus."

Some of the brave deeds executed by these war dogs were detailed. A liaison dog named Follette was seriously wounded on the Somme. Despite a violent barrage she managed to reach the commanding post of the colonel. Here, having accomplished her mission, she "died."

Forty-eight soldiers owed their lives to the war dog Pastou. A company of infantry were attacked by a superior force of Germans, and were threatened with encirclement. A three-fold barrage of fire precluded any chance of retreat. Three times the company commander detailed three scouts to get help. The men were killed in succession.

He then sent the dog Pastou with the message which told of the critical situation of the company. Pastou took eleven minutes to cover the distance of three kilometres (almost two miles).

Reinforcements were immediately sent by the major to whom the message was safely delivered. The forty-eight men who formed the remaining strength of the endangered company were relieved.

Yet another valiant dog was Medor who, in effecting a liaison under violent bombardment, was seriously wounded in the Battle of the Somme. In spite of these wounds, the dog continued his mission. Two days later he "died."

Some of these dogs have been mentioned in despatches, and decorated for their bravery.

For three years, under shot and shell, the Belgian shepherd dog Taki carried messages over the battlefields. She came through unscathed. Royal honour was accorded her. She also received the Croix de Guerre and other medals. Taki passed on in 1931 at the age of twenty-one, and was given a military funeral.

Apart from these canine war heroes, scores of dogs have won fame for acts which have saved the lives of human beings.

Bob of Carmel, an Alsatian, twice saved a man from possible "death." On the first occasion he dragged his owner, Mr. Durham, from a blazing car. The second time was when the same man slipped over the edge of a high cliff where, hundreds of feet below, the sea thundered against the rocks.

In a precarious position Mr. Durham clung to a small shrub growing on the cliff. He was afraid to hoist himself for fear of uprooting the bush, his only means of support. Bob came to his rescue by leaping on to a piece of rock just above the man's head. Reaching down, the Alsatian planted his feet firmly on the rock, and took Mr. Durham's coat collar between his teeth. Then the dog tugged upwards with all his might until his owner's rescue was completed by people who heard his calls for help. Bob's bravery won him a gold medal.

The "Dog's V.C." was an award instituted by the "Daily Mirror." This newspaper presented a number of canine heroes with collars containing silver badges inscribed "For Bravery." The dogs excited great interest when they were exhibited in a special corner at Cruft's Dog Show. Their deeds of valour were recorded in a pamphlet issued by the "Daily Mirror."

One dog V.C., a collie, finding the house on fire, aroused the family who were able to escape. Unfortunately, in the crowd, the dog missed his playmate, the baby. He rushed into the blazing building again, and was dragged out by the firemen; whom he attacked. Again he entered the burning building. A second and yet a third time he was rescued, only to rush back into the flames. Finally, he evaded the firemen and his charred body was later found in the ruins.

Gyp, a five months old puppy, also received the "Daily Mirror" V.C. for saving the lives of three children. His owner took his family on a camping holiday. One night, the tent in which the children were sleeping caught fire. The puppy rushed into the tent. To awaken the children he dragged the bedclothes off them. They were saved before the blazing tent collapsed.

Corkie, also decorated by the "Daily Mirror" for bravery, was owned by an old man, Mr. Ritchie, of Mid-Calder, Scotland. He was walking with the dog over the hills when they were overtaken by a snowstorm. Collapsing with the cold, Mr. Ritchie sank to the ground. Corkie stayed with him all night, lying across his neck to keep him warm. At daybreak, the dog ran off for assistance.

Cracker, another dog, saved the life of his owner's daughter. The child was seen by the dog to be clinging to the back of her father's moving car. In order to attract his owner's attention, Cracker threw himself repeatedly at the car. He "died" from the injuries he received, but his efforts succeeded in saving the life of the child.

Cats also have exhibited great courage in the face of danger. Here is one example recorded in the "Sunday Express." When fire broke out in the kitchen of a London house, the tabby cat, who was sleeping there, aroused the household by throwing herself repeatedly against the kitchen door and making it bang.

The animal could easily have jumped out of the open kitchen window, leaving the human occupants to their fate!

This notice appeared in a Buffalo newspaper:

"A cat, which rescued her family of kittens from a burning building, is to receive a certificate of bravery from the American Humane Association at a public ceremony. The mayor of the city, Mr. Tom Holling, is to officiate."

When called upon to do so, animals have exhibited and proved that they, as well as humans, possess the quality of courage. And, in common with man, they have risked, and sometimes sacrificed, their lives in deeds of valour and daring.

Faithfulness, self-sacrifice, loyalty—these are amongst the highest attributes in mankind. Man's spiritual nature is revealed in the great heights of selfless devotion reached by some human beings. But even in expressing these lofty virtues animals continue to share with humans similar qualities of the soul.

We may turn back the leaves of history and find records of ancient Greece and Rome, telling of the faithful devotion of dogs—or find similar stories chronicled in our modern newspapers.

The house of Alcibiades, the Athenian, was set on fire by his enemies. He tried to escape from the burning building, and was struck down by a hail of arrows. The dog by his side was mortally wounded at the same time. Forgetting his own injuries, the faithful hound tried to draw the darts from the body of his owner.

An even more touching story, handed down from ancient days, is that of the Roman, Titus Sabinus, who was thrown into prison for conspiracy. His little dog, refusing to move, languished outside the prison door. When the time came for Sabinus to be killed, his body was flung down the Germoniæ—the "steps of wailing." The dog followed and stood there howling piteously. Somebody in the crowd flung a piece of bread to the distressed animal. He picked it up and tried to force it between the lips of Sabinus.

Finally, when the Roman was flung into the Tiber, the little dog sprang into the river and swam to the body. Crowds of people watched the animal's pathetic but hopeless efforts to hold up the corpse and endeavour to bring it to land. At length, exhausted with his unavailing labours, the small dog perished in the Tiber.

Such faithful devotion has seldom been excelled by man—the"superior" animal.

Similar records of animals who remained faithful unto "death" come from all parts of the world. There is the story of the little Swedish dog who, in all weathers, lay for ten years on his owner's grave in Stockholm. Kindly people used to feed him at his place of vigil. Touched by the pathos of such devotion, somebody; finally built a little shelter for him near the grave of the one lie would not leave.

A drinking fountain was erected in Edinburgh to the Skye terrier Bobby as a tribute to his undying fidelity to the memory of his owner, a Midlothian farmer.

After his owner passed on, the dog followed the funeral procession and stood by the side of the grave while the service was read. The relatives of the "dead" man left, but Bobby remained lying on the ground. Here he was found the following morning by the sexton. He was turned away.

But, unseen in the dusk, he crept back that evening, to make his bed on the grave. Once again, he was expelled on the following morning. Once again, nightfall found him in the place where his owner lay.

Soon, the dog's tenacity of purpose became known to several people. A soldier from the neighbouring barracks used to provide an innkeeper with a weekly ration of steak for him. Regularly, at one o'clock every day, Bobby trotted off to the inn for his dinner. After his meal he would return to his lonely vigil. As the inn closed on Sundays, Bobby used to prepare beforehand for that day by hiding scraps of meat under a nearby tombstone.

In bad weather, many people tried to induce him to take shelter for the night. Such kindly efforts were unavailing. Bobby's home was with his "dead" owner—in a chill and comfortless churchyard.

Thus, fourteen years passed. One day, Bobby was found "dead" on the grave. The post-mortem examination of his body revealed he had cancer of the mouth. The disease was brought about by the damp bed on which he had chosen to lie for so many years.

"Greyfriars Bobby was buried in a little plot near the church, and a rose-tree was planted over the grave of this faithful dog.

In a daily newspaper there recently appeared the story of a dog who tried to lift his dying owner from the road where he had collapsed. Finding he could not raise the stricken man—an old rag-and-bone dealer—the dog licked his face and hands and then lay howling by his side. Until a doctor appeared and rendered assistance, the animal refused to allow anyone to approach.

There are many similar records of devotion and love shown by animals towards their owners.

Compassion is undoubtedly one of the highest spiritual expressions of mankind. Because Jesus of Nazareth manifested such an abundance of this tender quality of love, it may be counted as one of the most divine virtues man has developed in his evolutionary journey through the ages. Compassion is veritably an expression of the soul itself. Yet this aspect of love has manifested not only through God's highest creation—man—but also through the despised rodent, the rat.

Nina, Duchess of Hamilton and Brandon, told a meeting the story of a man who saw two rats running along together. He threw a stone which killed one of them. The other remained where it was. Upon investigation, the man discovered that the living rat was blind. It still held in its mouth the piece of straw by which it had been led by the other rodent.

A rather touching story appeared in "The Cat." The incident, which is well-attested, took place between two mother cats. All the kittens belonging to one of them had been taken away. In the box where they had been born, the bereft mother cried piteously. In another box in the same room was a more fortunate cat. She still possessed and fondled her own five kittens.

Distressed by the wails of the second cat, she picked one of her five kittens in her mouth. Then she carried it across the room and presented it to the grieving mother, whose cries promptly ceased.

Another story of animal sympathy also appeared in an earlier journal of the Cats' Protection League. A woman owned a cat named Minkie who used to play with a neighbouring cat. At the age of two, Minkie became totally blind. Constituting himself as a guide to the stricken Minkie, the other cat continued to call at the house and take him for a walk. Afterwards he would escort his playmate safely home again.

At séances all over the world, spirit beings, who have acquired great knowledge and understanding in the course of their evolution, return to earth to teach simple truths to those who will listen. They tell us that there is a part of the divine spirit in every living being. We are in God, they say, and God is in us.

The truth of these spirit teachings is proved by the fact that divine love and compassion are expressed even by God's lowliest creatures. There is no living creature which lacks the potentialities for developing and evolving. the higher qualities usually associated only with human beings.

When this truth is properly understood and appreciated by all of us, it will herald the birth of a new world—a world in which there will be no room for cruelty or oppression, either of man or beast.

CHAPTER V

THE SIXTH SENSE

MANY animals and birds have deeply rooted and inherent faculties of instinct. They often demonstrate an intuitive sense more highly developed than that of the average human.

Certain animals, particularly cats, have been known to find their way over long distances in order to return to homes from which they have been removed.

War has provided a number of astounding accounts of cats who found their way home after being sent away to avoid air raids. The animals were conveyed to the new quarters by various means of transport. They must of necessity have often covered entirely fresh territory when they made the return journey of their own accord.

On the outbreak of war, Mr. G. Jenkin motored his wife and family from their home in Surbiton to Ashburton, Devonshire, a distance of 180 miles. They were accompanied by Peter, their Siamese cat. Mr. Jenkin returned to Surbiton. Ten days later, Peter disappeared from his new home in Devonshire. And ten weeks later, he reappeared in his real home in Surbiton. His owner told a newspaper reporter that the cat was not hungry when he arrived. "Evidently Peter was fed up with evacuation and walked home," said Mr. Jenkin.

A "News Chronicle" contributor told how a cat was sent a distance of sixty miles away from her owner's home in a Cumberland village. The animal travelled in a covered van. A few days after arriving at her new destination, three kittens were born. The following week, cat and kittens disappeared. Three weeks later, the mother cat and her complete family arrived in the old Cumberland home. The writer said, "How she conveyed them is a mystery. The kittens were only able to crawl, and she could not have carried them more than one at a time—and there still remains the problem of food."

The "News Chronicle" reporter suggested that unless the cat "hitch-hiked" she must have walked three hundred miles, not counting extra journeys in search of food!

Yet another cat took two and a half months to accomplish a journey from London to Doncaster. She did this in order to rejoin her family of kittens.

Referring to the fact that hundreds of cats live on the sea, the same newspaper pointed out that they rarely miss their ships although they go ashore in different ports all over the world.

Ships' cats seems to develop a remarkable sixth sense. When the ship is in port they often go ashore, but they know when it is time for the ship to put out to sea again. Mr. J. Ford, who lives at Mill Hill, near London, gave an instance of one of these seafaring cats to the "News Chronicle." Tabby lived on board, but it did not matter if the ship put into a port for only half an hour, the cat would be first ashore. She never once missed rejoining the ship before it sailed. "Sometimes we would be in port for a week," said Mr. Ford, "and would not see her for the whole of the time, but just before sailing she would trot up."

The story of another remarkable journey made by a ship's cat was told in the "Edinburgh Evening Dispatch." This animal was greatly attached to the boatswain of the *Stuart Star* and usually slept in his cabin. When the ship was off Cocatoo Island, near Sydney, the cat went ashore, and on November 22nd, as the cat had not turned up, the ship had to sail without her.

On January 14th the *Stuart Star* arrived at the London Docks, and six days later the cat came aboard. She had travelled over 11,200 miles before she re-boarded her own ship! When she came on board, she went straight to the bo'sun's cabin to look for him. Unfortunately he had been put ashore at Freemantle, ill with appendicitis, but the cat was not satisfied until she searched the whole ship for her favourite. It is not known how she found her old ship.

The master of the *Stuart Star* said, "The theory is that the cat boarded the *Themistocles* or a Commonwealth and Dominion liner in Australia, and as we arrived in London about the same time she then recognised her old home."

But how did she know which ships were London bound? Was it a lucky chance, or did she exercise that curious sixth sense possessed by cats?

One of the strangest stories concerns Prince, the dog who, in the Great War, found his way from London to his owner in the front-line trenches of the British Expeditionary Force. So remarkable was this feat, that many people refused to believe the story when it appeared in the Press. But the R.S.P.C.A. took pains, at the time, to investigate the matter very thoroughly, and were able to confirm the published account.

In September, 1914, Private James Brown went to France with the North Staffordshire Regiment. He left behind him, in Ireland, his wife and his Irish terrier Prince. The dog, who was devoted to his owner, fretted for him, and refused to be comforted.

Shortly after her husband left for France, Mrs. Brown came to England and took Prince to her former home in Hammersmith, South-West London. About a month after her return to London, Prince disappeared. Every effort to trace the missing dog failed. In great distress, Mrs. Brown wrote to her husband in France, telling him of the animal's disappearance. To her astonishment, she received a reply saying that Prince had found his way to him in France.

How he made this extraordinary journey remains an unsolved mystery to this day. The fact remains that he disappeared from London and arrived, a fortnight later, in Armentières, where he suddenly appeared before an astonished Private Brown. He greeted his owner with the utmost affection, as though he had sought him out and was overjoyed at achieving his ambition.

The news quickly spread through the regiment. Private Brown and his dog had to parade the next morning before the commanding officer in order that the latter could prove for himself the reality of the fantastic story he had been told.

Prince was allowed to "settle down" with his owner in the front-line trenches, and quickly accustomed himself to his new life. He was a great favourite with the regiment, and his remarkable journey had earned him a reputation which was the envy of every other regimental mascot on the Western Front.

According to his owner, Prince was an excellent fighter who, in addition to bravery and intelligence, had yet another quality, that of caution. Whenever a heavy shell came over, the dog started off instantly, and never failed to take cover.

The dog remained in France until 1919, when the R.S.P.C.A. brought him safely back to England for his owner. Prince's portrait was afterwards painted for this society by Mrs. Shaw-Baker, who considers him the most famous of her many war dog subjects.

The homing instinct of some species of birds is highly developed. Numbers of pigeons are trained to carry messages over very long distances. At Arras, in France, a carrier pigeon was released to discover whether it would be able to find its way home to Saigon, Indo-China, 7,200 miles away.

The experiment was successful. The bird arrived at its home loft at Saigon twenty-four days later.

This is the most striking homing feat on record. The pigeon had travelled to France in a wicker basket in the hold of the ship. During the voyage around India, via the Red Sea and the Mediterranean, the bird had no opportunity of choosing landmarks; which might visually have helped it on the flight back to Saigon.

The civilised human being does not possess the strong instinctive and intuitive faculties manifested by animals.

Perhaps it is one of the penalties imposed by the ultra-civilisation of man.

But then, nature has struck a balance, for we in our turn have a cultivated consciousness, an appreciation of beauty, art and an intellectual ability superior to the animal.

Animals have frequently given examples of their ability to foresee the future. This strange psychic sense often functions before impending disasters, illness or "death." Although there may be a number of exaggerated stories about the howling and whining of dogs before a "death," there is, no doubt, a strong basis of truth in these tales.

In the "Daily Express" there appeared a story of a dog's foreknowledge of the impending "death" of his owner.

Police Sergeant Hebborn, of Beckenham, won a raffle. The prize was a wire-haired terrier. He was a grand little fellow, and a great bond of affection soon sprang up between the man and the dog. Whenever the sergeant came home from his police duties, a bark of welcome from Tim would always greet him. One day, the police sergeant had a slight accident whilst cycling, and had to return home.

"From that moment Tim changed," Mrs. Hebborn told the newspaper representative. "He never barked again. He began to see things. He would rush about the rooms of the house and stare. I believe Tim could see the Angel of Death in the house."

When her husband became worse, the dog, in a kind of daze, lay under his owner's bed, and refused to move. He neither ate nor drank. When the man became unconscious the dog seemed to go into an entranced condition. He left the sick room and went out of the house. Mrs. Hebborn heard afterwards that Tim went in and out of the police station three times, walking through all the rooms as though searching for his owner.

Later, the dog returned home. He seemed to be unconscious of his surroundings. If Mrs. Hebborn moved his head or his legs they remained limp. Tim would make no movements of his own volition. She took him to Mr. Cornish-Bowden, a veterinary surgeon, who could find nothing organically wrong when he examined him. The dog did not move even when a needle was inserted in him and an injection was made. "His symptoms," said Mrs. Hebborn, "were just the same as those of my husband, who had developed pleurisy and meningitis." The vet kept the dog for the night, and two girls sat up to take care of him.

The wife learned afterwards that as her husband lost his sight, hearing and feeling, the dog also lost these senses! When morning came and the sick man passed over, Tim "died" at the same time.

"I believe he knew what was to come," Mrs. Hebborn told the reporter. "That is why his collar is to be laid in the coffin."

I have quoted this story, not because it is a touching instance of an animal's love, but as an indication of a dog's premonition. Nobody thought that a slight cycling accident would have resulted in "death." But Tim knew, and such was the bond of love between the dog and the man that Tim took on his beloved owner's symptoms and then followed him into the next world.

Her own experience of animals' psychic intuition, was told me by Miss Lind-af-Hageby, the famous humanitarian. During her work in France in the Great War, she was taken over the battlefield of the Manse in a conveyance drawn by two horses.

Suddenly, and for no apparent reason, the animals stopped dead and refused to continue in the direction they had been making. She was told, afterwards, that horses, killed in the war, were buried beneath the soil over which the living ones refused to travel.

I remember reading about a man whose dog howled persistently on certain days. He could never discover the reason. His house was near a lethal chamber, and he found out, one day, that the howling of his animal coincided with the times that dogs were being "put to sleep."

Once, when some theatrical friends of mine were on tour, their dog absolutely refused to cross the road in a certain town where they were staying. Although they tried to persuade him to leave the kerb, he drew back, howling piteously. The animal's unusual behaviour interested my friends. They made inquiries in the town and discovered that, a few hours previously, a dog had been run over in the same road.

A bird's mother love for her fledgelings, and her foreboding about their fate, led to forceful, tragic behaviour on her part. In human life, such fatalistic acts have provided many a fruitful theme for classic drama on a grand scale.

In "Progress Today," E. Douglas Hume related the following authentic story about a rosella, a native parrot of New South Wales. These birds are often caught and kept as pets.

A man robbed a rosella nest of three fledgelings. He caged them and put them on a wagon with the intention of selling them in Sydney. The mother-bird followed the wagon for over two hundred miles. Through the bars of their cage she fed her fledgelings with grass seed and grubs.

The time came when, had they been free, they would have been old enough to leave the nest. At this stage, the mother-bird perched on a tree some distance away from the wagon, and called loudly to her young. But, alas, they were unable to obey her summons.

Something then seems to have told her that they were helpless prisoners, with no chance of escape. She flew away, returning later to feed them, apparently in the same manner as before. But there was a subtle and tragic difference in the last meal she brought. The seeds must have been gathered from a poisonous weed, and the three little captives dropped "dead."

"Wise little sorrowing mother!" wrote Douglas Hume. "Intuition must have warned her of the fate of many so-called 'pets.'"

It would be difficult, indeed inconsistent, to ascribe the mother-bird's act as one of "instinct." Instinct, which had led her to follow and successfully nourish her young for a distance of over two hundred miles, would not suddenly have played her false. No, one must search deeper for an explanation—an explanation that lies outside purely physical realms.

When I told this story to a friend, she recalled a similar instance which happened in her house. Having found an injured fledgeling thrush she kept it on a shelf in the living-room, hoping that eventually it would recover and be able to fly away. Meanwhile, the mother-bird used to fly fearlessly in and out of the living-room to bring tit-bits to her injured offspring.

Unfortunately, one day, my friend had to leave the house shut up and unattended. A cat got into the living-room by the window that had been left open at the top for the mother-bird to visit the fledgeling. A neighbour, unable to get into the locked house, told my friend a strange story. She saw the cat trying to reach the fledgeling, which became terrified. Agitated, the mother-bird fluttered vainly about the room. Then she flew out of the window, and came back with something which she forced between the beak of the frightened fledgeling.

The next moment the young bird lay "dead." The mother had forced a poisoned weed between its beak! Apparently, she preferred to take its life herself rather than let it succumb to the menace of the cat's claws.

A case which may, or may not, have a physiological explanation rather than that of pre-knowledge, is told by Henny Kindermann about the talking dog, Lola.

When Lola was going to have puppies, her owner, in fun, asked her several days before the event how many offspring there would be. Lola, in her language of raps, told her there would be nine puppies. And, sure enough, nine there were!

She had also forecast how many males and how many females she would have. She was only wrong in one instance—not a bad "guess" on her part.

In "Animal Life" appears the story of a cat's premonition and intelligence.

A woman who owned an apartment house had a guest who was lying ill. The sick woman's constant companion was a large black cat. One morning, the owner of the house was awakened by a gentle pull on her hand. It was the cat, who conveyed that she wished the woman to accompany her.

The animal led the way to the sick woman's room—she was breathing her last. A moment later, she was "dead. Disconsolately, the cat sat by the body...

CHAPTER VI

PASSING UNDERSTANDING

THERE are a number of people who, knowing nothing of the facts of Survival, consider themselves too superior to acquire any knowledge of the case. They will airily explain away all clairvoyance as "telepathy between the medium and the person receiving the spirit message."

The reality of telepathic communication has been fully established, and no thoughtful person nowadays questions the fact. But when thought-transference is instanced as a denial of communication between the living and the "dead," Spiritualists usually smile. Telepathy is a fact which helps to *prove* the case for Survival, not to deny it!

Telepathy involves communication between minds without the use of our sense organs. It reveals that mind is superior to matter, for telepathy has been successfully demonstrated when the experimenters were separated by hundreds of miles. Why should the death of the body mean the cessation of the mind? Since the mind is superior to matter, there is every reason to suppose—apart from psychic proofs—that it continues to function after "death" and can still practise telepathy. This time, however, thought-transference is conducted between a discarnate and an incarnate mind.

Telepathic ability is developed more strongly in animals than human beings. By their behaviour, domestic pets have given definite proofs of the reality of thought-transference between themselves and their owners. As is always the case where a sympathetic love exists between an animal and a human, this affinity stimulates the animal's ability to contact the mind of the human.

Miss L. K. Schartau, the Secretary of the Animal Defence Society, and an indefatigable worker and enthusiastic in this progressive organisation, has been kind enough to provide me with an experience of thought-transference between herself and a beloved dog.

She writes, "In a dog-lover's life there is, I have found, one special dog, who stands apart from other beloved dog friends, who plays a part in your life unlike that of the rest, who means to you something which you hold sacred and which cannot be put into words. Such a dog was Mono to me. Mono began life as the friend and mascot of a Canadian flying officer—hence his name Mono, short for monoplane.

"He was a Welsh terrier of the old type with large and luminous eyes which often arrested passers-by and drew admiring comments from them. But besides his beauty and charming, gay manners, he had, for his few best friends, a deep love which made him count for nothing his own pleasures and comfort in order to be close to them in times of sickness or sorrow.

"How he came to our home at the age of three is a story of sad adventure, too long to relate here. The important thing is that he came and stayed with us for nearly thirteen years, until one dark evening his spirit slipped away and left us grieving by his still, worn body."

Miss Schartau goes on to say that Mono's great intelligence was apparent from the first days he came into her environment, but, coupled with his marked high mental ability, she found that his mind was capable of receiving, and acting upon, her thoughts of him. She first discovered this telepathic sense through an experiment made by her in her anxiety for his safety.

Miss Schartau lives in the neighbourhood of Primrose Hill, London. Years ago, of course, there was considerably less busy traffic in that neighbourhood than there is today and Mono was allowed out by himself, to play on the far side of the hill, two or three minutes' distance from his home.

His habits were very regular, and half an hour was his average time for roaming at his leisure. After that time, he would return home and would always go straight upstairs to Miss Schartau's room and tap on the door for admittance.

But one morning, she suddenly noticed that the tap at her door was long overdue, and, in view of his usual regularity, she began to feel concerned. As she was not yet dressed and could not go out immediately to look for him, she wondered whether a mental call to him would have any effect. She stood perfectly still and, concentrating on the missing dog, she repeated mentally, "Mono, come to me at once, I want you."

Within two or three minutes, there was the familiar tap on the door. Mono had returned.

On reflection after the incident, however, Miss Schartau felt inclined to dismiss the dog's return after her mental call to him as a pure coincidence. But another time came when Mono was late in returning from his play. Once again she sent him a similar mental request to come home. Within the time it took him to leave his favourite haunt, the dog returned. After that, if ever the dog stayed away too long, he never failed to return within a few minutes of her telepathic message to him.

Being a reasonable, intelligent woman, Miss Schartau was forced by these circumstances to change her mind as to the "pure coincidence" of the animal's actions.

She also mentions the fact that, when she sent him a mental message to come home, she never noted the time by the clock. She only called him when she realised that he had overstayed his usual half an hour. Sometimes it would be thirty-five to forty minutes, or even longer, before she became aware that he was overdue. It is interesting to note that, on the occasions when he returned home after a mental call, he arrived in a breathless condition, quite different from his ordinary leisurely manner.

"It suggested that he had suddenly become aware of the urgency of returning home, and he raced at top speed," writes Miss Schartau.

She gives yet another instance of Mono's strong mental link with her. Miss Schartau would leave her office at irregular hours. The time of her return home was regulated by her work. Nevertheless,

Mono always took up his position in the hall, by the front door, about half an hour before her arrival. This was the approximate time it would take her to make the journey from the office.

She points out that her maidservant, by no means given to psychological speculation, was struck by the daily recurrence of Mono's behaviour, and it was she who first drew attention to his actions.

One day Miss Schartau arrived home at an unusually early hour. She was surprised to find there was no dog to greet her, and was told that the maid had taken him for a long walk in Regent's Park. "Ten minutes later," says Miss Schartau, "an excited Mono came tearing up the road and hot in pursuit, a very breathless girl. `Well I never,' was all she could gasp."

After she had regained her breath, the maid told of Mono's strange behaviour. When, on their outward journey, she and the dog were nearing the lake, Mono, who had previously been running gaily in front of her, suddenly stopped dead for a moment. Then, turning, he sped home as fast as he could run, ignoring the calls of the maid who chased excitedly after him.

Later, on verifying the time, Mono's sudden halt and subsequent race for home coincided with Miss Schartau's arrival at the house. She points out also, that "no dog ever enjoyed a good walk more than Mono. He was always loath to turn back home."

Although in this instance, the dog did not, for some reason or other, sense the time Miss Schartau started on her homeward journey, it would appear that he caught her thoughts when she arrived home to find he was not there with his usual greeting.

In the interesting book about the educated dog Lola, to which I have referred in previous chapters, the author tells how she discovered that Lola caught her thoughts telepathically. She noticed that when Lola was tired, or lazy, the. animal would express her owner's thoughts instead of using her own powers of individual thinking.

There are some cases of mental communication between man and animal that are usually accepted as telepathy. They could, however, be just as easily explained by the theory that a message to the human has been transmitted by spirit agency. But, in either case, all thought-transference may be considered a psychic faculty, since it involves the transmission of messages by means of communication outside the usual range of the five senses.

The famous novelist, Sir Henry Rider Haggard, received, in a dream state, the impression that his dog lay dying. The details of the story appear in the journal of the Society for Psychical Research.

The author's wife heard her husband groaning in his sleep, emitting sounds like an animal in pain. He told her later that he had experienced a dream which, on his being awakened, became increasingly vivid. The author said he had seen the dog lying on his side amongst brushwood by the water's edge. His own personality, he said, seemed to arise in some mysterious fashion from the body of the dog, who lifted up his head at an unnatural angle against his owner's face. "Bob was trying to speak to me," declared the writer, "and not being able to make himself understood by sounds, transmitted to my mind in an undefined fashion the knowledge that he was dying."

The morning after the "dream," Bob's blood-stained collar was found on a railway bridge. Four days later, the animal's dead body was recovered. It was battered and broken. Bob had been struck by a passing train and the impact had thrown him from the bridge into the water beneath.

Mrs. Macneil Dixon told the following story in the "Daily Mail."

While on holiday in Paris, she received a letter from her husband written from India. He said that her cocker spaniel was ill with tick fever. She telegraphed for further news and received by return a cable saying that the dog was better. "The following night," said Mrs. MacNeil Dixon, "I awakened about 3 a.m. with the strong conviction that my dog had died. At 8 a.m., I received a cable confirming her death. On my return to India, I found that my dog had died practically at the moment when I had awakened that night."

Mrs. Hewat McKenzie, who founded, with her husband, the British College of Psychic Science, has given me an interesting supernormal experience concerning a goat.

Here is the story in Mrs. McKenzie's own words:

"We were residing in the country and were the possessors of several goats who were sometimes tethered during the night on a piece of grassland about 300 yards from the house. One of these was a large white goat. My husband had been confined to the house for some weeks through illness and could only give directions to the gardener daily as to the animals.

"We also possessed at this time a dog, a large powerful Dane, and strict orders were given that it was to be carefully chained up each night in case of trouble.

"One morning when I awoke, my husband informed me that he had had a curious dream or vision. He had found himself out in the grounds and had seen the white goat lying on its side, dying, with its belly torn. He knew at once this had been caused by the Dane.

"The gardener came for orders about 7.30 a.m. and he asked me to send him up at once and to say nothing about the dream. I did so and stood by while they talked. Asked if everything was all right with the animals, the man seemed uncomfortable.

"My husband, noting this, said, 'Now I am going to tell you exactly what you found.' He proceeded to relate his dream, to the man's evident astonishment, for he knew that Mr. McKenzie was forbidden to leave his bed because of a disabled leg. He confirmed every detail. The goat was dead and the Dane had broken his chain.

"Was this telepathy from the animal? There was no affection established here as might have been with a dog, though when well my husband often cared for the animals. Even if the calls of the animal had reached him in bed—this was not very likely unless he was more sensitive owing to his illness—this would not account for his seeing himself standing by the goat and noting its condition.

"His own conclusion was that he had been temporarily out of his body, the only experience of this kind, in relation to his earthly surroundings, he ever claimed. My children and other friends were well acquainted with the incident at the time it happened."

Another explanation which might apply equally well to the

other stories of this type is that spirit agency was used to attract the human's attention to the animal's plight.

I do not know which is the true inference. But it is certain that the operation of a supernormal law is involved.

• • • • •

I have endeavoured, by logical argument, to present the case for animal survival.

Also, I have given attested accounts proving that animals have independent minds. I have shown that, in common with mankind, our lesser brethren possess mental attributes that do not perish with the death of the physical body.

The same natural law operates in both cases.

For illogical and generally unjust reasons, we humans are often loath to give animals their rightful due when they display similar mental qualities to ourselves.

When, for example, a human mother makes a supreme sacrifice on behalf of her child, she is rightfully applauded for her selfless act. But when a four-legged creature makes a similar sacrifice for its young-well, we often dismiss it as a touching display of "animal instinct."

Really, no distinction should be drawn between identical altruistic behaviour, whether it be made by a human or by an animal.

What is instinct? None of us exactly know.

In any case, I see no reason why an act of altruism should lose value because it springs from a desire, so deeply rooted, that the response is automatic.

The instinct for good, as well as for evil, must first have been a conscious desire, before use and habit formed the conscious wish into an unconscious or involuntary action.

Self-sacrifice on the part of an animal is no more and no less commendable than human self-sacrifice. Comparisons that belittle and dismiss as "instinct" the altruistic acts and the virtuous qualities in animals are not consistent, unless the same conclusions are drawn in regard to human behaviour.

CHAPTER VII

PETS WHO LIKE SÉANCES

THERE are animals who like to be present at séances. They behave quietly and well during the sittings. Cats, particularly, seem to be interested in the supernormal. When the traditional witch rides through the night on her broomstick, or casts her magic spells over the boiling cauldron, the cat is never far away!

In my home we hold a weekly circle where we talk to our guides and friends on the Other Side. Often, before the sitting is due to begin, my cat, Paddy, will wander restlessly about the room, examining and looking at things we cannot see. He deeply resents being put into another room.

Paddy is not as fortunate as the little Pekingese who belongs to a friend, the wife of a foreign diplomat. When husband and wife hold their séances, Sally is permitted to remain in the room.

They obtain spirit messages with the help of a table. This kind of séance is an easy method of communicating with those who have passed on. The sitters arrange themselves round an ordinary wooden table, lightly placing their fingers on its surface. When there is sufficient psychic power emanating from those present—and there usually is, especially when the sittings are held regularly—the "dead" are able to communicate by tilting the table and spelling their messages by means of an alphabetical code.

Sally greatly enjoys being present at these sittings. Moreover, she insists on lying comfortably on top of the table. As it tilts—so does Sally! But she remains calm and unperturbed throughout the séance.

Sally, from whose tiny form exudes a tremendous personality, has led an unusually exciting and varied life for a little pet dog.

She has lived in several European countries that, in the past few years, have been in stages of upheaval or conflict.

I first made the acquaintance of this little dog in Barcelona, where my friends lived for many years. When my husband and I joined them there with the intention of spending a quiet, peaceful holiday, we found ourselves in the midst of the Spanish Revolution!

After five days in Barcelona, the four of us decided that it would be advisable to leave Spain. We visited the British Consul and the Catalonian authorities, and had our papers put in order.

We decided to make for the French frontier in our cars. It was arranged that, because our friends could speak Spanish, they would lead the way in their car, and we would follow closely behind.

To her owner's distress, we had to leave Sally in Barcelona, in charge of their trusted Catalonian servant. It was not considered safe to take the dog on our hazardous journey through a country in a state of civil war.

And what a journey it was! I do not think I shall ever forget it.

Altogether, our two cars were halted at seventy-six different barricades where, each time, the armed guards who blocked our progress, challenged us at the point of their rifles. With their country at civil war, they were only doing their duty, but these continual halts were rather an ordeal. Moreover, we experienced one or two very unpleasant incidents when our friends were nearly shot before our eyes.

On the first occasion, through misunderstanding a signal, they did not respond quickly enough to the challenge to halt at a barricade. My husband and I were horrified to see the guards level their rifles at the car. Frantically, we sounded the motor-horn to attract their attention and, fortunately, they stopped in time!

How they escaped from being shot the second time would be called a "miracle" unless one knew, as we did, that it was due to spirit intervention. This time it was late at night. It was a favourite trick of escaping insurgents to dazzle the guards at the barricades with their car headlights and then flash past them. Instructions had been issued that no headlamps were to be used. Unfortunately, we had not received these orders, and consequently, the lamps of both cars were burning brightly.

Soon, the headlamps of our friends' car showed we had reached a barricade. To our consternation, we saw the guards raise their rifles, and take aim at them. We had a moment of horror—but the guards did not shoot!

We all stopped and the guards asked why we had not complied with the regulation about the headlamps. Then one of them made a significant remark. "Why you were not shot, I do not know," he said. "Just as I was about to pull my trigger, *something stopped me*."

Normally, it was only a day's journey through Spain to the French frontier. But the constant delays had considerably checked our progress. When, late at night, we were still travelling towards France, I began to feel a little nerve-racked with the strain of that day.

It was at the moment when my courage began to falter that I felt a warm, comforting but unseen han.. clasp mine. The materialised hand, as physical in touch as a human one, gave me renewed strength.

Before we started on our journey we had had a sitting, when our spirit communicators assured us they would be able to protect us, providing we did not give way to fear. When we reached the safety of the French frontier, we mentally thanked our unseen friends for the protection they had given us.

While Spain's civil war was in full swing, my friend was moved by his Government to Berlin. As it later transpired, it was a case of "out of the frying pan into the fire"!

After some months in Germany, he received permission to return to Spain to settle his affairs in Barcelona. He was able to take Sally back to Berlin to rejoin her beloved mistress.

Shortly after the present war broke out, they were again moved to another country. This time it was Denmark. Then he was recalled home just before Germany decided to take Denmark under her "protection.." But always, in whatever part of the world they happen to be, they keep in touch with the spirit world.

Although I have not seen them for some time, I have no doubt that Sally still continues to take her see-saw rides on top of their séance table.

Mr. Walter Wilson is secretary to Mrs. Gladys Osborne Leonard, well known as Sir Oliver Lodge's medium.

Sometimes, it is her secretary's duty to have what is known as a "proxy sitting" with the medium. That is, on behalf of a person who, for certain reasons, does not wish to attend, the secretary will take notes of what transpires. Incidentally, these "proxy sittings" are the complete answer to the "telepathy between sitter and medium" theory which is supposed to explain away evidence for Survival.

Mr. Wilson had a much-loved dog named Philip who was sometimes allowed to remain in the séance room when his owner took notes at the sittings. The dog would remain calm and patient during the whole time the medium's guide was in control.

But he always knew when she was coming out of trance. As, by stages, she returned to her normal self, Philip would get up, yawn and stretch himself. "He *knew,*" Mr. Wilson told me, "that she was `coming back' and that the tedious period of being quiet was over."

Although the dog has now passed on, his spirit form still comes to them when his owner is having one of his "proxy sittings" with Mrs. Leonard. Sometimes Feda, the medium's guide, will break off in the middle of a sentence to say to Mr. Wilson, "The white dog is here. He is on the couch, in front of Gladys."

CHAPTER VIII

PSYCHIC ANIMALS

SOME houses are haunted. We are all familiar with stories of "ghosts." They are, in truth, spirits of people who are earthbound—their etheric bodies are chained to this earth for some reason or other. Often, a crime they have committed holds them to this physical plane; sometimes jealousy or greed ties them to their earthly home. In some cases, they do not even realise that they have undergone the change called death.

Spiritualists hold séances to help free these spirits from the links that hold them to their former abodes. Whilst they are earthbound, their spirit bodies are dense, and are even visible to people who do not possess clairvoyant sight.

Animals can also see them. They often show emotion and fear at the sight of one of these unfortunate beings, caught between two states of existence. A cat's hair will stand on end, and a dog will howl and show the utmost terror in the presence of one of these tormented earthbound souls.

But animals do not usually show the same terror when they clairvoyantly see those who have passed over and who return to earth for a brief spell to visit their loved ones.

Animals, because they are more psychic than humans, often see those who are invisible to us. Indeed, so clearly do some animals discern spirits, they cannot always differentiate between the living and the "dead."

Several people who have visited the home of Mrs. A. E. Deane, the psychic photographer, will confirm this fact.

When a psychic photographer takes a picture of a living person with an ordinary camera, there often appears an "extra" on the plate. The image of a "dead" person has impinged itself on the photograph of the living one. Hundreds of "dead" people have been recognised and acknowledged by those who have sat with Mrs. Deane for psychic photography.

Mrs. Deane has an unusual hobby for a psychic. She breeds St. Bernard dogs, and has been a well-known exhibitor at Cruft's Dog Show where some of her enormous pets have won high awards.

St. Bernard dogs have very affectionate dispositions. Once or twice when I have visited Mrs. Deane, I have been almost *too* overwhelmed by their demonstrative greetings. When one of these huge, lovable animals has jumped on his hind legs to put his enormous paws on my shoulders, I have nearly lost my balance.

Spirit people, invisible to so many of us, have often been so clearly seen by these dogs that they have mistaken them for people of this world.

My husband, as well as other people who have called on Mrs. Deane, has sometimes witnessed a strange spectacle. He has seen one of her St. Bernards bound forward to greet an unseen visitor. The dog has jumped up on his hind legs, and, when his front paws have passed through space without meeting the solid resistance he expected, the animal has looked most surprised and bewildered.

There are scores of well-attested instances of animals having seen spirits. In "Human Personality And Its Survival Of Bodily Death," F. W. H. Myers, the famous psychic investigator, recorded the case of a donkey who, apparently, saw the spirit of a child. The narrative was communicated to the Society for Psychical Research by Mr. E. A. Goodall, of the Royal Society of Painters and Water Colourists.

Whilst in Italy, the artist decided to move from a seaside resort to another town. In order to facilitate his journey to Ischia he rode a donkey. In his report, Mr. Goodall describes the animal as "one of the fine, sure-footed, big donkeys of the country."

The painter goes on to say, "Arrived at the hotel, and whilst sitting perfectly still in the saddle talking to the landlady, the donkey went down upon his knees as if he had been shot or struck by lightning, throwing me over his head upon the lava-pavement."

A few nights after this accident, which caused a certain amount of injury, Mr. Goodall awoke from his sleep to the sound of an unrecognisable voice telling him that his youngest child had passed on. This disturbing psychic incident was followed by letters from his family in England informing him that his youngest child had been taken suddenly ill, and had "died."

As nearly as Mr. Goodall could judge, the "death"' of his child coincided with the time of the accident he had sustained by the donkey's fall.

He believes that the sudden fall of this usually sure-footed animal, could only be explained by its terror at the unexpected appearance of the spirit body of the child.

Both humans and animals take their own personalities through the gates of "death." The act of dying does not change the character of the individual whose body has been discarded.

Captain J. A. Godley had a schipperke dog named Peter who was his constant companion for fourteen years. Some time after the dog passed on, he was accurately described to his owner by a medium. Peter was not at all sociably inclined towards other dogs. When out walking with his owner, any dog who approached would be rebuffed by his ferocity.

Some time after Peter's passing, Captain Godley saw, in the street, a friend approaching with his little cairn terrier, Judy. This dog was fond of the Captain and usually greeted him affectionately. But when he stopped to speak to his friend on this occasion, Judy deliberately avoided him and ran into the road. Later she returned gingerly to the pavement, but still kept about ten yards away from Captain Godley.

Because he would not have been understood, Captain Godley did not explain the reason for Judy's unusual behaviour. He realised that his "dead" schipperke was accompanying him on his walk. The little cairn was avoiding the fierce, gleaming teeth of the spirit dog. Still jealous of other animals who approached his beloved owner, he continued to display his earthly behaviour.

Here is another example, as told to me by a Mrs. Wheatcroft who returned to live in the home of her childhood. She brought with her a cat she had owned for the past three years.

As soon as she took up residence in the old home, her cat, who had not, of course, lived there before, behaved in an extraordinary manner. He refused to stay indoors for any length of time, and would suddenly fly out of the house. Only with difficulty could he be induced to come in again.

This behaviour went on for some time. His owner could not understand it until, one day, she saw clairvoyantly the spirit form of a big collie. She recognised the dog as Jerry, the pet who had lived with the family when she was a child, and was obviously still attached to his old home.

When Mrs. Wheatcroft realised that the cat could also see the spirit dog and was frightened of him, she behaved very sensibly. She welcomed the dog, but told him he must not frighten her cat, who was a newcomer to the old house. Jerry understood, for since then the cat has settled down happily and comfortably.

The spirit dog still visits his old home but only when the cat is out. So everybody is happy!

Mrs. Wheatcroft is fortunate in being psychic, for although she is alone all day she says she never feels forlorn. She is often able to see clairvoyantly her "dead" husband. Sometimes he brings a dog named Laddie who belongs to them both and who has also passed on. She has never seen Jerry and Laddie at the same time, but she often wonders what would happen if they both paid her a visit together.

Personally, I think that those on the Other Side would, whenever possible, prevent two jealous dogs from meeting, in the same way as we would separate two animals who did not agree. So perhaps Mrs. Wheatcroft has no cause for alarm!

I remember an acquaintance, a retired doctor, telling an interesting story about his favourite dog. When the animal was alive, he always sat under the same chair at the dining-table.

Some time after he "died," the doctor got another dog. One day, their new pet sat under the same chair-but not for long!

He had only just made himself comfortable when, with a flying leap, he left his position. Then he stopped, and looked in a most puzzled manner at the place he had left so hurriedly.

It was obvious from his behaviour that the "dead" dog was not very far away and was guarding the rights to his own special seat.

CHAPTER IX

HOW THEY RETURN

ALL kinds of domestic pets have returned after "death" and given unchallengeable proofs of their continued existence in another sphere.

In addition to these higher animals even some of the more lowly creatures have also returned to demonstrate the fact that they still lived.

They have manifested their survival through different channels of mediumship. Scores of animals have been described by mediums to their owners at public Spiritualist meetings.

Sometimes the spirit descriptions have come as surprises to members of the audience who had gone perhaps with the thought of getting a message from a "dead" relative or friend. They have been none the less delighted by the unexpected joy of a description of a "dead" pet.

At private sittings with mediums many persons have received proofs of the continued survival of animals.

"Dead" pets have returned to their delighted owners at séances held in the privacy of the home, where no professional medium has been present.

By means of psychic photography, animals who have passed over have reproduced their likenesses on photographic plates in the same way as hundreds of humans have done.

I believe that "dead" animals are helped by spirit people to give proofs of their survival in more or less the same way as "dead" children are assisted by older and more experienced spirits. Even on earth, this is usual, for children and animals need more help than adults.

At materialisation séances, the sitters have seen and felt the "solid" forms of animals who have reproduced their earthly bodies using the ectoplasmic substance drawn from the medium.

Some psychics are "voice" mediums. By means of an ectoplasmic larynx, the "dead" speak in a reproduction of their earthly voices which can be recognised by those who knew them. Often at these séances, a light "trumpet"—a cone-shaped megaphone—is placed in the room and this is used by the spirits to amplify their voices.

The trumpet usually floats in the air. It is attached to the medium by psychic "rods," invisible to the physical eye. If a séance is held in the dark, part of the trumpet is treated with luminous paint so that its movements can be followed.

The dexterity displayed by the spirit operators in moving the trumpet in the dark, in a crowded room, is a source of wonder to me. Although we ourselves cannot see, the trumpet will move unerringly to the person to whom the spirit wishes to speak.

Sometimes, the spirit operator will make remarkable movements with the trumpet that could not be done without difficulty by earthly people. Sometimes, the trumpet will touch the ceiling, and in a split second will next be seen on the floor. These gymnastics in the dark are sometimes done by spirit intelligences to convince an honest sceptic that supernormal power is functioning.

One of the usual taunts directed against Spiritualism by our opponents is that séances are held in the dark and this condition enables the "mediums" to produce fraudulent phenomena. Actually, the majority of séances do not take place in the dark.

White light is destructive to certain types of physical phenomena, such as materialisation and direct voice. These séances, therefore, are either held in red light or in complete darkness, except for the luminous trumpet.

This can be easily understood when it is recognised that these phenomena are analogous to the processes of birth. The germination of life takes place in the dark. Seeds have to be planted in the darkness of the earth. It is in the absence of light that they begin their growth.

In like manner, the growth of the human and animal embryo takes place in the darkness of the body. Remember, also, that wireless reception is more successful during night time. White light has a deleterious effect on photographic plates, which can only be developed in the dark or in red light.

In any case, it is neither the presence, nor the absence of light at a sitting that matters. It is the evidence received that is the only test.

I have attended hundreds of physical phenomena séances, many of which have been held in good red light.

I have been present at direct voice séances where the barking of a "dead" dog has been recognised by a sitter as the characteristic sound made by the animal on earth.

Often, after a dog has thus greeted his owner through a trumpet, the spirit guide in charge of the proceedings has volunteered evidence about the animal that has given the sitter further proofs of his identity.

Every well-developed medium has a spirit guide or control.

At direct voice séances, the guide helps the spirit people to speak when they are in difficulty. During trance sittings a guide will speak through the lips of the medium, whose own consciousness is temporarily laid aside. The medium's body and actions are thus fully controlled by the guide.

It will be appreciated that only highly evolved spirits are elected to act in this capacity. Their function is to protect the medium and to be a kind of doorkeeper for all the spirit people who come within the medium's orbit.

In addition to a guide, a psychic will sometimes have one or more spirit controls. Whereas guides are highly evolved beings, controls are selected for their ability to co-operate with the guide in producing psychic manifestations.

We have had in our home circle many different forms of psychic phenomena. In fact, at one time or other, we have experienced nearly all the "gifts of the spirit" that are referred to in the Bible—trance, control, clairvoyance, materialisation and the direct voice.

Sometimes, during materialisation phenomena, we would hear the sound of a "dead" dog's tail thumping on the floor in a delightfully realistic way when we greeted him. "Dear old Bint," the medium's husband would say to his "dead" pet, and "Thump, thump, thump," went the tail excitedly in response to his welcome.

Sometimes he would rub his head against his owner's legs. The medium's cat, Mickey, simultaneously with the dog, would also demonstrate his materialised presence by scratching with his claws on the carpet. This sound was similar to that made by any ordinary earthly cat. Fortunately for the owner of the carpet the effect was not so disastrous!

During some of our sittings, we have heard the chirping of a materialised bird. The sound of its fluttering wings could be clearly heard as it flew about the room. Sometimes it would come to rest and perch near one of the sitters.

There is a rather touching story attached to the first arrival of the spirit bird in our séance room.

Although our circle has since been rearranged, at one time the séances used to take place at the home of a medium, a gifted, cultured woman, through whose splendid psychic powers we received most of our physical phenomena.

One evening, when we arrived at the house in time for the weekly sittings, we found a somewhat tearful and sad medium.

She and her husband had been for a walk during the afternoon, and picked up a fledgeling which was lying injured on the ground. Apparently, it had fallen from its nest. They took the bird home and did what they could to preserve its life. But despite their efforts, it soon "died."

Regretfully, they made an improvised coffin in which they placed the tiny bird. They buried it in their garden, and covered the grave with leaves. The tender-hearted medium then said a prayer for the soul of the fledgeling whose earthly life they had been unable to save. This little ceremony had just been completed when my husband and I arrived at the house. Later, we went to the séance room for our usual sitting.

After the medium had gone into trance, we were surprised to hear the unmistakable chirping notes of a young bird,' and the fluttering of its wings.

We were all very happy when the spirit guide in charge of the circle spoke to us afterwards and explained what had happened. He told us that the love showered on the fledgeling and the sincere prayers made on its behalf, had called forth from the soul of the bird an individual consciousness. The guide said that, because of this human contact, the spirit of the bird was able to manifest in the materialised body that had returned to say, "Thank you!"

The bird often manifested at subsequent sittings. With the dog and the cat, it was always a very welcome visitor.

Scores of well-known people have been invited, at different times, to attend our home circle. These people, whose integrity and intelligence are beyond question, have testified to the truths of the physical phenomena they have witnessed.

• • • • •

Just when I had finished this chapter, I went to one of the most remarkable voice séances I have ever attended. The evidence simply poured through. The medium was Mr. Kenneth Hillberry. In addition to personal proofs vouchsafed to me, Mr. Alfred Timson, one of the sitters, received unexpected evidence of the survival of his dog.

Through the trumpet, the medium's Indian guide, White Fox, addressed Mr. Timson.

"There is a dog here for you," he said. "His name is Rough. He is a black sheep dog. You brought him home from school."

This was acknowledged by the sitter to be perfectly correct. He told me after the séance that he had never met the medium before, and was almost overwhelmed with this and further evidence of Survival he received that night.

He said that when he was a schoolboy he picked up a stray puppy and took it home. The puppy, a black sheep dog, was named Rough, and passed over several years ago.

CHAPTER X

PHYSICAL PROOFS OF SURVIVAL

I HAVE attended many direct-voice sittings held by Mrs. Estelle Roberts, the famous medium, whose psychic gifts have done so much to convince sceptics of the truths of Survival.

At one of these séances I heard a "dead" retriever named Lon greet his owner, Dr. Margaret Vivian, by barking through the trumpet.

Dr. Vivian has had many interesting psychic experiences in connection with this intelligent dog who passed on in 1918. Lon has demonstrated his continued existence to his owner by varying methods and through different channels of mediumship.

Dr. Vivian has told in "Psychic News" how she received news of the dog a few months after his passing. By means of a planchette, operated by an acquaintance, she had a spirit message from a great friend who had passed on. This communicator, whom she calls "F.R.," said to her, "I have your dog. It cannot find a way to communicate with you directly. I want you to know that death is not the end of all. Whenever you have the sense of needing him, your dog answers."

Dr. Vivian asked "F. R." where her dog was. He replied, "I have him. He is with you often. In time you will realise it and respond in every way, as you already do in your heart. He will survive until you also come here, and after. Quite special care is taken of your dog and of others by those who, like myself, have always loved them."

He went on to say, "I am Lon's guardian always. He is with you in all that matters, and always will be. Have no fear of his ever losing you; though you have, for the time, lost him, it is merely transitory."

Dr. Vivian said that she asked "F.R." to help her find a medium through whose power the dog would be able to show his materialised form. "Several years later," she says, "through two different mediums, I saw my dog's materialised form for a few fleeting seconds, and felt his feathery tail beating against my knees."

The spirits controlling these manifestations told of the great difficulty they experienced in getting a dog to "hold the form." Dr. Vivian explains: "Lon is a black retriever, and white dogs are easier to see in the dim red light of a materialisation séance."

If ectoplasm is not competently held together by the spirit form using it, the body crumples up and the form has to be "built up" again.

Referring to the effect of human affection on Lon's condition on the Other Side, Dr. Vivian records that "F.R." said, "His [Lon's] high standard of spiritual health, the wide measure of freedom your dog has now attained, is due to your unrestrained affection for him, which gave him a greater consciousness and courage."

Various animals have manifested their presence at materialisation séances held by the famous Polish medium, Franek Kluski. The mediumship of this cultured man of many artistic accomplishments has been investigated by well-known scientists. There is a considerable amount of literature concerning the psychic powers of this medium.

In describing the materialisations at the Kluski sittings, Professor Pawlowski says in "Psychic Science," "The most frequent visitors of the animal variety are squirrels, dogs and cats. On one occasion, a lion appeared, and on another a large bird like a hawk or buzzard."

He goes on to say that the animals behaved in a perfectly natural way. He describes how he saw the materialised form of a dog "running about, wagging his tail, jumping on the laps and licking the faces of the sitters, and responding to the more or less universal code used among people with trained dogs."

The professor also speaks of the buzzard which would fly around the room, beating its materialised wings against the walls and the ceiling. Once, this bird was photographed with the aid of a magnesium flash. This photograph is reproduced in Dr. Gustave Geley's "L'Ectoplasmie et la Clairvoyance."

In "Psychic Science," Mrs. Hewat McKenzie speaks of the same bird in her references to Colonel Ocholowicy's book on Franek Kluski. She says that, before the bird was photographed, the sound of its whirring wings could be heard.

"This sitting," writes Mrs. McKenzie, "was held in the light of a red lamp, fixed about six feet from the medium. In this the outlines of a grey moving mass were visible, but could not be distinguished as a bird, this fact only being ascertained after the plate had been developed."

She also refers to an Afghan who used to materialise at some of Kluski's séances, and would bring with him an animal who seemed to be rather like a maneless lion. This animal would "lick the sitters with a moist and prickly tongue, and gave forth the odour of a great feline, and even after the séance the sitters, and especially the medium, were impregnated with this acrid scent as if they had made a long stay in a menagerie among wild beasts.

The animals that materialised through this remarkable medium's gifts varied from the savage variety, such as the lion, to the most gentle, attractive types of undomesticated animals.

Perhaps the object was to prove that all living creatures survived and retained their. characteristics, although no doubt the more savage type of manifestation was held in control by protecting forces.

A grave, dignified Eastern spirit visitor to the Kluski séances was always accompanied by an attractive little animal which looked like a weasel. "Its behaviour was always gentle," writes Mrs. McKenzie, "and the sitters were very fond of it, trying to hold it near them as long as possible. But as soon as the human apparition with it vanished, so did the beast.

"It used to run quickly over the table on to the sitters' shoulders, stopping every moment and smelling their hands and faces with a small cold nose; sometimes, as if frightened, it jumped from the table and rambled through the whole room, turning over small objects and shuffling papers lying on the table and writing desk."

With another medium named Guzik, Mrs. McKenzie tells how Sir Oliver Lodge, Professor Charles Richet, Dr. Gustave Gelsey and other scientific investigators all recorded "careful impression of what seemed the manifestation of an animal like a dog, which fondled some of the sitters, and pushed its nose into their pockets."

This highly intelligent woman, who has had a vast and varied experience of all kinds of psychic phenomena says, "If great animals appear, such as have been seen at Kluski séances on occasions, then we may reasonably suppose that the domestic animals, so often dearly loved, are at times not far from their owners, although opportunities for objective manifestation may be lacking. There are hundreds of well-attested cases of persons, seeing, hearing, feeling and sensing the presence of deceased pets in the ordinary home surroundings; the behaviour of other animals has also seemed to indicate a knowledge of unseen companions."

A dog once materialised sufficiently strongly at a séance to bite the shoe laces and trouser legs of his owner.

This incident was vouched for by Mr. Christopher Harrison, of Ongar, who described it in "Psychic News." He tells how a little boy, who looked about four years old, also materialised at this sitting. The child called out, "Doggie, doggie" and explained that he had brought the dog to the séance, and that he was looking after it on the Other Side. While all this took place, the medium was in a deep trance in the "cabinet" which is used at most materialisation séances.

A "cabinet" is usually made by hanging a curtain, across the corner of the room, behind which the medium sits. This separation from the other sitters allows the medium's ectoplasm to "build up" without the interference of other people's vibrations. When the ectoplasm is "built up" sufficiently strongly for the spirit forms to materialise, they usually come outside the cabinet while the medium, of course, remains inside the curtained space.

I have, however, often seen a fully materialised spirit control draw aside the curtain and the two figures, the spirit form and the medium (usually in a deep trance) have been visible at the same time.

In America I attended a séance given by Mrs. Ethel Post, a well-known medium. In this case, and in good red light, her guide, a young Indian girl, came out of the cabinet and walked the whole length of the room, a distance of thirty feet. She talked with some of the sitters at the furthest end of the room. This guide invited my husband to stand up and accompany her back to the cabinet. Then he was asked to go inside to make sure that the entranced medium was still there. He satisfied himself on that score and was able to see both the medium in the cabinet and the guide outside—at the same time.

When a discarnate being is able to materialise completely, the counterpart of the physical form is reproduced, including the organs that compose the body and help it to function. This means, of course, that heart and lungs are temporarily reproduced and function naturally, as long as the psychic power is sufficiently strong to hold the materialised body together.

Scientists have recorded heart and pulse beats of discarnate beings during these physical manifestations. Sir William Crookes, the famous scientist, cut a lock of hair from a materialised being. These spirit forms have been known to drink water.

I have seen a spirit child eat a sweet. You may ask, "Where does this earthly substance go after the spirit form has dematerialised?" Because the spirit form is "built up" from ectoplasm emanating from the medium, it is generally assumed that the earthly substance consumed by the spirit disintegrates and becomes absorbed in the medium's body.

A well-known medium, Mr. Charles Glover Botham, used to hold a materialisation home circle where, on one occasion, the sitters were very surprised when a materialised form of a large dog suddenly appeared. He bounded forward in a most energetic manner and proceeded to jump excitedly about the circle. Wagging his tail happily, he ran from one sitter to another, resting his paws on their knees and sometimes licking a hand or a face. The animal seemed thoroughly to enjoy the amount of affection and interest displayed by the members off the circle, most of whom were great animal lovers.

But the crowning point of this remarkable psychic demonstration was yet to come. This happened when the dog ran to a bowl of water that was always provided at the séances for psychic purposes. Often, at this type of sitting, water is placed in the room. It is said to aid the conditions because it contains psychic energy.

The materialised animal proceeded to lap up the water eagerly and noisily as though the excitement had made him thirsty. Afterwards, the bowl was found to be completely empty. There was not a drop of spilled water to be seen anywhere.

Psychically one of the sitters received an impression of the name "Hector." Mr. Harold Sharp, another medium present, recognised Hector as being a favourite dog who lived on his parents' farm. Hector had been a great pet of his "dead" mother, who was also accurately described to him at this sitting. "This was the first description of my mother I ever received," Harold Sharp told me.

Later, through different mediums, his mother returned and gave him further evidence which revealed the fact that she continued to spend much of her time in the spirit world amongst the animals she loved when on earth.

At another sitting held by Mr. Botham, a Siamese cat materialised in quite good light. The cat jumped from one sitter to another, and allowed itself to be stroked. It rubbed its head affectionately against the faces of the circle members.

Another instance of evidence through materialisation, and in the direct voice, is provided by Mrs. D. Montague Smith, who volunteered these facts to me. There was a bond of love between her and her Great Dane, Buller, who passed on twenty-five years ago. Mrs. Montague Smith regularly attends direct voice séances with the medium Mr. Ronald Strong. Her dog has often returned to her and barked with joy through the trumpet. "And there is no mistaking his deep bark," says his owner, who ought to know! Once, Buller materialised so successfully that he placed his great paw quite heavily on her arm. During the fifteen years she has been a Spiritualist, this dog has been described to her by three different mediums.

The combined psychic gifts of two sisters, the Misses Moore, have provided much evidence of Survival through their direct voice mediumship.

The Rev. V. G. Duncan, a Church of England clergyman, has had a number of sittings with these mediums. He tells in his book "Proof" how he heard a woman receive evidence of the survival of a dog and a cat. At this séance, the spirit guide, Andrew Wallace, addressed Mrs. Stewart, one of the sitters. "D'ye no have a dog here an' he belonged to ye?" he said in his broad Scottish accent. "His name is Rex."

Mrs. Stewart answered that this was perfectly correct. "Can you tell me what he looks like, Andrew?" she asked. He replied, "He's a wee white doggie wi' a smoothish coat. Dinna ye ca' them fox terriers?"

Mrs. Stewart agreed that Rex was a fox terrier. "Aye, went on Andrew, "and there's a wee cat that belonged to ye here as well. D'ye ken thot?" The sitter replied that she had lost a cat for whom she had much affection.

"That's it; ye had it a lang while," went on Andrew Wallace. "Oh, yes, for seventeen years," agreed Mrs. Stewart. She said that she had often wondered whether cats and dogs survived after they had passed on.

The spirit voice of Andrew told her, "Aye, they live as lang as yer love lasts for them. After thot they go to their ane place." "Well, there's no mistake about them being alive now, " answered Mrs. Stewart. "It's marvellous."

The Rev. V. G. Duncan describes how they later heard the barking of the dog, and the mewing of the cat, as the materialised forms of the animals ran round the circle. "We felt them brush against our legs in unmistakable animal fashion and the cat tried to clamber on Mrs. Stewart's lap," says the clergyman.

This combined voice and materialisation manifestation must undoubtedly have rejoiced the heart of the woman whose "dead" pets demonstrated so adequately the fact that they still survived.

"From being an agnostic, I became a Spiritualist largely through the remarkable sittings I had with the late Cecil Husk," says a writer in "Psychic Science." He tells how, when he sat with this materialisation medium, the spirit form of his sister, a nun, used to come to him.

On one occasion, she brought his dog, who had recently passed on. This large hound barked naturally. The owner, who was allowed to stroke the animal's materialised body, states, "The feel of his coat seemed to be like that of the dog I had lost, and its reaction was as if it were delighted to be caressed."

Through the direct voice mediumship of Mrs. Etta Wriedt, Mr. Ernest Hayward, O.B.E., and his wife became aware of the continued survival of their dog and a favourite Persian cat. Mr. Hayward has served the Admiralty in many countries, and has achieved distinction in this service.

In "Psychic Experiences Throughout the World," of which his wife is co-author, he tells how they spoke to their "dead" son Brenton at a sitting with Mrs. Wriedt. He asked his son whether it was true that there were horses in the next world. Brenton replied, "Yes, Father. It is like this. We have all the animals that we love. Horses, dogs, cats and birds-only in etheric form."

At a later sitting their "dead" daughter Cecily said she had brought Kouss-Kouss, a Persian cat to whom she had been very attached when they were both on earth.

"Shortly after," write the authors, "we heard two sneezes and a bark through the trumpet. Cecily told us that it was our little fox-terrier, Sandy, who had been killed in Malta." Mrs. Hayward asked the dog to bark, as she wanted to be sure that it was indeed her "dead dog. At her request, the dog gave a sharp bark through the trumpet. When she asked him again to "give a louder and stronger bark" the animal immediately responded.

A couple of years later, they attended a séance given by the materialisation medium Mrs. Helen Duncan, and were again able to see the built-up form of their "dead" dog. At the same sitting their daughter Cecily materialised. She gave proofs of her identity and convinced her parents that she was aware of events that had happened to them since her passing.

Then Cecily said she was going to give them a surprise. The

authors write, "And sure enough the curtains of the cabinet opened and Sandy, our little fox-terrier which we had all loved so much, appeared outside. He turned his head from side to side and pricked up his ears alternately as if curious to know what was happening, After sitting for a minute or two he disappeared."

How her guide kept a promise to prove the survival of a dog was told me by Mrs. Lilian Bailey, of Crewe, one of the finest mediums in the Spiritualist movement. Her Pekingese passed on after being the pet of the family for thirteen years. The medium told me, "Chin was really uncanny in her knowledge of our human language. She would even try to 'reply' to us. Chin would give sharp, staccato barks if we praised her."

Mrs. Bailey has, as one of her spirit controls, a little girl who is known as Poppet, who promised that she would help to bring Chin back to prove, beyond doubt, that this beloved Peke still lived. Months later, Mrs. Bailey was invited to attend a séance given by Mrs. Helen Duncan.

To the joy of Mrs. Bailey, Poppet fully materialised at this sitting. Mediums who work under condition of trance do not often have the pleasure of talking to their own guides in the séance room. They are naturally always delighted when they receive this rare opportunity.

Mrs. Bailey says, "Out of the cabinet came my little control, bearing in her arms the form of a dog. 'I have brought Chinnie with me,' she said. I called to the little dog and it disappeared out of the child's arms. But from the cabinet came the short, sharp barks of excitement I knew so well. We could hear Chin careering wildly around.

"Truly, Poppet had kept her promise," adds Mrs. Bailey, "and proved to me, beyond all doubt, that the beloved little dog still lived. I look forward with great joy to meeting Chin again one day.

Some time ago, Mrs. Bailey gave trance clairvoyance at a public Spiritualist meeting at Leicester. Though they were scattered throughout the hall, her guide correctly singled out the members of one particular home circle. Mrs. Bailey had only arrived in Leicester half an hour before the meeting. The people were strangers to her and she could not have known anything about the circle they had formed. Since her visit to Leicester, this circle has begun to develop direct voice phenomena.

When Mrs. Bailey was in London, I asked her if she would send me particulars of her experience of Chin's materialisation so that I could record the evidence in this book. While she was preparing her account for me at Crewe, she received a letter from Leicester which she forwarded to me with her promised contribution.

The letter to the medium says, "I do not know if you remember your visit to the Leicester Society for Psychic Research when your guide spotted member after member of a circle."

The writer goes on to describe how, at their circle on the previous evening, Poppet spoke to them. She told them she had brought "a curly doggie" with her. As far as they could tell, she gave the dog's name, which sounded like "Shoots."

Mrs. Bailey fully understood this message given by her guide at the Leicester circle, for, she tells me, "My father, years ago, had a fine curly-haired retriever named Shot. It was a fine dog whom we all adored for its almost human instincts."

I agree with Mrs. Bailey that Poppet apparently heard the two of us discuss this book on animal survival. The control must have decided that she would try to help me by providing some further evidence through a different channel than the one she generally uses.

To meet this adorable little spirit control is to love her. It is typical of her good heart and goodwill to try to help others.

CHAPTER XI

MENTAL PROOFS OF SURVIVAL

WHEN the son of Mr. Holland Hennequin died after a motor-cycling accident, his father decided to investigate Spiritualism. The results he obtained, recorded in "Psychic News," were considered by Sir Oliver Lodge to be "practically perfect."

Through several mediums, Mr. Hennequin received evidence of animal survival. His son Eddie spoke to him at one sitting with Mrs. Annie Brittain and gave a message from Ted, the "dead husband of a woman friend. Mr. Hennequin asked the medium's guide, Belle, whether Ted still had his dog with him on the Other Side.

"What, the one that is yapping all the time, and keeps jumping up to him?" Belle asked. "Eddie says he can hardly hear himself speak because of it."

Mr. Hennequin then asked the guide, "What is the dog like, and what is its name?" Belle replied, "It is a little rough, long-coated, yellow dog, and its name is Pimp."

This was an accurate description of the "dead" dog. "It was a light yellow, long-haired Yorkshire terrier," confirms Mr. Hennequin, "and the name was Pimp." Ted was convinced that he would meet his dog when he passed over. When he lay dying, Ted looked at his dog's photograph and said, "All right, Pimp, I shall soon be with you now."

At a later sitting with the same medium, Mr. Hennequin received some information about his own dog who was lying ill at home.

"Eddie says you are going to do something you have never done before," Belle told the sitter. "Something has been worrying you lately, but you have now made arrangements that will leave you more free to leave the house, and you can now go away and shut the door and have no cause to worry."

This was all true. Mr. Hennequin had never been away without his dog before. Because, that year, the dog was too old and ill to travel, he had been worried as to the best thing to do in the circumstances. Eventually, he arranged that somebody should go and live at the house and look after the sick dog whilst he was away.

"Please ask Eddie if he remembers Dinkie," said Mr. Hennequin to the guide. Belle replied, "He says something about a paw. He is making a sign with his hand like a paw. I think Dinkie must be a dog."

"Yes, he is," agreed the "dead" boy's father. "He says Dinkie is not well."

"He is very ill," said Mr. Hennequin. And he asked Belle whether they could not try, on the Other Side, to help the dog to get better.

Declaring that she was speaking for Eddie, Belle replied that they had tried to help the dog but that he would not get well. "You might patch him up for a time," the sitter was told, "but he has run his course. He is too old."

Mr. Hennequin agreed that this was indeed the case. "Dinkie will soon come over to you," he said to his "dead" son. "When he comes, will you find him and keep him for Mum and me until we come?"

"You leave it to me," said Eddie. "He won't leave me once he finds me again. I will look after him and get him back into good condition, and you will find him wagging his old tail when you arrive.

"I must look after him," continued the boy. "He was my dog, and will be the first of the old home to come over. I can't build my home in this world until I get someone from the old home to share it. When he comes, he will share my home here until you and Mum come, and then it will be all ready for you."

Dinkie's health rapidly deteriorated. His owner considered it was cruel to keep the suffering animal in this world, and he had him peacefully "put to sleep."

Some time later, Mr. Hennequin and his wife had a sitting with a different medium, Mrs. Kathleen Barkel. Her guide is White

Hawk, a North American Indian, whose lovable disposition and fine sense of humour are known to the many Spiritualists who, with his help, have received evidence of the survival of their loved ones.

At this séance, Mr. Hennequin asked whether the shaking of his dining-room door a few nights previously had been due to a psychic manifestation by Eddie.

"No," said White Hawk through the lips of his entranced medium. "That was Dinkie… Eddie brought him home to let you know he was with him. The little dog got too eager, and ran to the door and scratched at the bottom of it."

The guide then asked Mrs. Hennequin whether she missed the dog.

"Yes, very much," she answered.

"Hold your hand here," said White Hawk. The medium, controlled by her guide, took Mrs. Hennequin's hand, and held it about eighteen inches from the floor.

"Do you feel a cool breeze blowing to and fro?" asked the guide. "That wind is caused by the dog wagging his tail because he is pleased to see you."

Mrs. Hennequin exclaimed, "This is wonderful; I can feel it!"

Her husband's hand was then taken by White Hawk, and held in the same place. He, too, felt the psychic breeze caused by the dog.

All this was evidential to the sitters, because no mention had been made by them about having lost their dog. Indeed, they had made no reference to a dog at all until White Hawk spoke about their own animal.

When they told the guide why they had been obliged: to have Dinkie "put to sleep" he replied, "I understand. He will not be ill any more. He is full of life. He runs about the fields with Eddie."

White Hawk then asked, "Do you know a spirit named Ted?"

"Yes," answered Mr. Hennequin.

"He is here," said the guide. "His little dog is a terrier, eh?"

"Yes," agreed Mr. Hennequin, "a Yorkshire terrier."

"I can see a little yellow dog run towards Dinkie," said White Hawk. "Dinkie crouches down as he comes, ready to spring."

Mr. Hennequin considers that this undoubtedly referred to the "dead" Ted Wheeler's dog Pimp, whose name had been given correctly to him at his sitting with Mrs. Brittain. The little scene described by White Hawk was typical of the way the two dogs used to play together in Mr. Hennequin's garden.

The guide asked Eddie's mother whether she had heard a sound of a dog's whimpering the other day.

"Why, yes I did," she replied.

She and her husband had both heard the sound, and they had agreed how much it resembled the whimpering of their "dead" dog.

"That was Dinkie talking to you," White Hawk told them.

Animals sometimes show themselves quite unexpectedly to mediums in between clairvoyant descriptions that are being given of "dead" humans.

Some Spiritualists wanted to help a sorrowing friend by trying to give her some knowledge of the facts of Survival, as she was ignorant of the Spiritualist case. They asked a mutual acquaintance whether she knew of a medium who would call at their house and give a sitting at which they would arrange for their friend to be present.

A medium named Mrs. Hester Lines visited them for this purpose. They had never met her before, nor had they even heard of her existence. The medium went into trance. Miss Jessie Palmer, at whose home the sitting was held, says, "The minds of the sitters were centred with deepest interest on the evidence which poured forth for the one who so needed the help."

After the guide had been speaking through his medium for some little time, he suddenly broke off to tell Miss Palmer that a spirit dog had just come into the room. "The dog is like the one you have here, but is bigger, with a longer tail, and one white paw," he said, and then gave even further details of the animal's appearance.

From this accurate description, Miss Palmer recognised the "dead" pet as their present dog's companion, one of the same litter in fact. Their dog had been devoted to Judy and, when she passed on, he always insisted on sleeping in her vacant box.

Sometimes physical peculiarities provide evidence of anima survival. Mr. Herbert Gregory had two fox terriers who passed on within a couple of years of each other. Mediums have accurately described these animals, both at circles and at public meetings.

On each occasion, a few weeks after the death of the dog, Mr. Gregory was told, in perfect detail, what the animal looked like, its colouring, and the markings on back and head. Because their owner disapproved of docking, these fox terriers had the full length of tail with which nature had provided them, and not the little stump most of this breed have after they have been docked. The mediums commented on the full-length tails of the animals when describing them to their owner.

Mr. Gregory also owned a whippet who, since his passing, has also been described to him. The medium referred to the plaid coat and collar the whippet used to wear before he passed over.

Giving clairvoyance to a woman at a Spiritualist meeting, Mrs. Florence Thompson described a cat named Jimmy who had been brought by the woman's "dead" father. The medium said that the cat's tail was shown to her shortened, bound round with a bandage because, when on earth, he had been run over by a cart wheel which had severed part of the tail.

The recipient of the message recognised the description of the cat and acknowledged the details to be accurate.

Of course, disabilities are shown to mediums in order that they may give evidence to the person they are addressing. It does not mean that the deformities continue in the next world.

The physical body has an etheric or astral counterpart through which the spirit manifests after "death." But if, owing to an accident, illness, or hereditary cause, the physical body is imperfect, the astral counterpart is unaffected. Disabilities are only temporarily reproduced by the spirit for purposes of recognition.

On another occasion Mrs. Florence Thompson told a woman that her spirit sister had brought a parrot with grey, green and red plumage. The recipient recognised this as an accurate description of her parrot Joe who had passed on. The medium then went on to remind Joe's owner of the occasion when the bird had pulled a lace curtain from the window into his cage and torn it to shreds. To punish Joe for his misdeed, she had moved his cage, for a time, to the other side of the room. This incident was immediately recalled and acknowledged by the woman in the audience.

The same medium once described a "dead" horse to a man. Although the man was in mufti, she said that he was a soldier who had served in India where the horse was accidentally shot. She told him of his affection for this animal and how deeply he had grieved when the accident occurred.

The man acknowledged that all the details were correct, and was delighted to receive proof that his equine friend still lived—and remembered him.

CHAPTER XII

COMFORTING THE MOURNERS

WHEN an unknown man once came for a seance with Mrs. Stella Hughes, one of the best-known mediums in the Spiritualist movement, she described a dog she clairvoyantly saw with him. Her accurate description of his beloved dog was the climax to a moving story which he told with tears in his eyes.

For years he had been a lonely man who, in his earlier years, had endured great hardship. He had been brought up in an orphanage. Because of the hard knocks life had dealt him, he grew into a lonely, bitter bachelor. He had never given love or affection to anybody, and in consequence he never knew the joys of friendship.

By sheer grit and hard work he rose to a good position in life. He became an overseer whom everybody found unsympathetic. People felt no attraction towards him either in business or private life.

One day, alone as usual, he was walking in the street, when suddenly a puppy, yelping in agony, flung itself against his feet. The animal had been injured by a passing vehicle in the road. In its terror and shock, the puppy rested its head on the man's feet, and gazed up into his face with a mute appeal for help.

Its trusting eyes softened the man's heart to sudden pity. He looked down at the puppy wondering what he could do. Then, making up his mind, he carefully gathered it into his arms. He had no knowledge of animals, but a friendly policeman led the way to a veterinary surgeon who lived nearby.

After inspecting the puppy's injuries, the vet told the delighted man that they were not serious, and that the dog ought to be well in a couple of weeks.

But, like himself, the puppy seemed to be alone in the world. Nobody came to inquire about him; he wore no collar, and had nothing to indicate to whom he belonged.

"If nobody comes to claim him by the time lie is well, you had better take him yourself," said the vet.

And so, at the end of three weeks, the man called and took the unwanted puppy to his own home. They became devoted friends, for they were two lonely beings who had found companionship.

Because of the dog, life took on a new meaning for his proud owner. He noticed, for the first time, that there were beautiful flowers and that the grass was green. When, on their numerous walks, the dog made friends with children, the overjoyed owner gave them gifts, a change for a man who had been miserly in his habits.

For fifteen years he enjoyed the friendship of his dog, who had turned him from a lonely recluse into a humanitarian.

Then, tragedy of tragedies, the dog "died." The sun went out of his life and all was dark. Friends tried to console him—for he had friends now. "Don't worry," they said, "there is another life for pet dogs."

This was the story that he tearfully related to Mrs. Hughes after she had described the dog, whom she said she had seen an hour before the man arrived. And, as further proof, she told him of incidents that had occurred in the days when the dog had made its home with its master.

The medium had removed his great ache. Psychic knowledge had given him comfort. For he knew that when his time came to pass on, his faithful friend would be the first to greet him.

Mrs. Hughes's splendid psychic gifts have been the means of proving that animals live after "death" to hundreds of their owners. It may be because she herself is so attached to animals that she is an ideal medium for their return.

Once Peter, her seventeen-year-old corgi, was ill. For four days he could not walk. "Why don't you have your dog 'put to sleep'?" a friend asked. But somehow she could not bring herself to end his earthly life. There was always a chance that he might recover...

Another medium telephoned her. "Your spirit guide has been to see me," she told Mrs. Hughes, "and asked me to pass the message on to you that you are not to have your dog destroyed. Instead, he wants you to give him psychic healing. Put your hand on him for five minutes, then leave him and when you return from the Queen's Hall, where you are giving clairvoyance, you will find Peter will be all right."

And when Mrs. Hughes returned home from the meeting she saw Peter running up the street!

Six months later Peter became ill again. This time Mrs. Hughes heard her own guide say, "Now put him to sleep." Still she hesitated. Later that day her friend, the other medium, telephoned again with a message from Mrs. Hughes's guide. This time he confirmed what he had already told his medium, "You must put your dog to sleep." With a heavy heart she obeyed the request.

That night when she was giving clairvoyance at another meeting, she saw Peter's spirit form running up the aisle. He was in fine condition, well and strong again in his new state of existence.

Mrs. Stella Hughes has a friend whom she always called Pauline. Pauline was devoted to her dog. One day the medium could not get rid of the feeling that the dog was going to pass on.

That same evening when another medium, Mr. Kenneth Hillberry, who knew Pauline, called, she told him of her impression. "Why do you feel the dog is going to die?" he asked. "He *is* dead!" A few minutes later the telephone bell rang and a distracted Pauline announced,. "My cairn is dead."

Later that evening a séance was held in the home of Mrs. Stella, Hughes. Mr. Hillberry's guide asked her to give this message to Pauline: "Tell Jessie that John has got her Biddy."

Though Stella could not understand this message she transmitted it to Pauline, who was delighted. Her real name was Jessie and John was her father, who on earth had been very attached to their cairn, Biddy.

Once, when giving clairvoyance at a public meeting, Mrs. Stella Hughes, clairvoyantly saw a cat without a tail. Psychically she received the information that the cat had lost its tail because someone had accidentally shut a door on it. When she gave this message, the recipient immediately acknowledged its accuracy.

Then there was a woman who, when she came for a sitting, was not surprised when this medium said she could see three peacocks with her—and gave their names, "Juno, Juniper and January." The woman told the medium that she was very fond of these three peacocks who used to adorn her Irish estate.

A barrister and his wife regularly came for séances. They had two unusual pets—a couple of frogs. One cold winter they both "died," and husband and wife felt sad about their loss.

When, some time later the barrister "died," his wife came to Mrs. Stella Hughes for a sitting. The medium was not only able to prove that the "dead" husband was present but moreover described the two frogs which she said came with him. She even told the surprised sitter the names of the frogs—"Adam and Eve." This was true, for the barrister and his wife had chosen these Biblical names for their strange pets.

It is interesting to note the way in which Mrs. Hughes psychically received these names. They came in pictorial form, for she saw clairvoyantly an old-fashioned picture of Adam and Eve in the Garden of Eden.

Mrs. Hughes also tells the story about Bob, a collie, she had in the country, who won lots of prizes. She had to leave him when she came to London. One day she said to her husband, "Bob's dead. He's been shot. I can see the bullet wound."

Later there came news that, because of old age, Bob had been shot at the time the medium had her vision.

Giving clairvoyance in London, Mrs. Stella Hughes once described a dog to a woman in her audience who had come up to Town for a few days. The medium was also able to give her the dog's name, Rags. But when she said the dog had been run over by a butcher's van, the recipient of the message shook her head.

"I have no knowledge of such a happening," she declared. Two weeks later, when she returned to her home in the country, she learned that Rags had been run over by a butcher's van during her absence.

When Mrs. E. M. Williams had a sitting with Mrs. Stella Hughes, the medium said: "A big black cat has jumped on the table beside you, and I am being shown a penny." Mrs. Williams understood. She once had a beautiful black cat named Penny. When he was a tiny kitten somebody had cut off his tail, leaving only a stump.

"Can you see his tail?" she asked the medium. "Yes," came the reply. "He has a very fine tail." Then she added, "My goodness, they are showing me his tail cut off!"

Not only has Mrs. Stella Hughes seen and described scores of cats and dogs to their owners, but also more unusual pets. Once, she saw clairvoyantly a monkey, and was able to prove that his passing was caused by being burned.

Then, too, she has clairvoyantly seen a donkey, and proved the accuracy of her psychic vision by pointing out that this animal only had one eye when it was on earth!

Mr. R. H. Saunders, a Spiritualist of considerable knowledge, who has now passed on, has told many interesting stories of animal survival.

In "Psychic News" he wrote, "When Mrs. Blanche Cooper, who is a great animal-lover, was giving séances at the British College of Psychic Science, it was quite a common incident for dogs and cats to materialise, and to be handled for a few minutes."

He also told of his collie dog which over fifty years ago had to be destroyed. Once, it manifested at a séance. Mr. Saunders wrote, "It gave a joyful bark when I called out its name and, as I fondled it, I felt its coat gradually melting under my hands."

A friend of his had two birds who were great pets. In course of time they "died." Years later, his friend's daughter also passed to the Other Side. Her father attended a séance at which the "dead" girl spoke to him. She said, "The two birds we were so fond of are here with me, Daddy."

At another séance with the same medium, Mrs. Etta Wriedt, her guide said to one sitter, "There's a horse here belonging to one of you," at which there was a laugh.

The guide, with some asperity, said, "You may laugh, but let me tell you that people here have their horses, dogs and pets. Ah! you little know the spirit world."

Mr. R. H. Saunders continued, "There are few who realise that, when we stroll out with our dog, we are accompanied by other dogs who have passed away long years ago. For once the bond of affection has been forged, it cannot be broken.

"In Spiritualism only do we get conclusive evidence that the soul—the spirit force permeating all nature—does survive. The link between us and our lesser brethren is maintained in the full beauty of reciprocated affection, and given suitable conditions, can manifest to us.

"There are the various realms to which all life gravitates at the dissolution of the flesh: human beings to their respective spheres, animals to their kingdom, birds to theirs."

There are cases to prove that even many years after their passing dogs have returned to demonstrate that they retain their affection.

Mrs. A. M. Williams's dog had "died" over forty years previously, yet she immediately recognised a medium's description of him. This happened during a circle when, in spite of the fact that she was seated close to the fire, she felt an unexpected chill round her feet and ankles.

Then she realised it was a "psychic breeze," the invariable accompaniment to some spirit manifestations. The medium told her of the presence of a beautiful big black dog and described how the animal went to Mrs. Williams and laid his head on her feet. Then, after gazing into her face with a wealth of love, he settled down comfortably to sleep.

Mrs. Williams not only recognised the medium's description of her dog but what was more important was the fact that the animal always behaved like this to her and to nobody else.

Another dog returned after forty-eight years. She was Nellie, who was speedily identified by her owner, Mr. Gilbert J. Nicholls because the medium described Nellie as "a white terrier with black ears."

Even when the purpose of a séance is not to obtain proof of animal survival, it is often volunteered by the spirit communicators.

A dog belonging to Mrs. B. M. Franks passed over after fifteen years' loving companionship. The dog's owner writes, "At a sitting where the first grief at our recent loss was very great, my father came through and I said, 'Where is Togo?' My father answered, "The little white dog is with me when he isn't with you."

Although she had not asked for evidence, it had been volunteered, *for the dog was white.*

Mrs. Franks says that the dog is still seen running about the house by members of the family. They hear him bark, and often hear the sound of his feet pattering down the tiled passage. "When my youngest daughter comes home," she writes, "I have heard his bark greet her before her arrival has been made known to us. We know our half-blind and totally deaf little friend is now quick and alert in mind and body."

Mrs. D. Cash owned a spaniel for over ten years, and when the time came for the animal to pass on she said good-bye, with sorrow, to her faithful friend. Some time afterwards, she was at a séance given by a medium in Bournemouth when her "dead" brother said to her, "Whom do you think I have brought with me?"

She at once thought of their father and mother. She was, therefore, very surprised when her "dead" brother said, "Old She."

"The dog's name was Sheila," says Mrs. Cash, "but we often used to call her Old She. The medium had no knowledge whatever of this."

Mrs. Bertha Harris, a well-known medium, described Mr. John G. Findlay's "dead" wife to him. She added that, his wife had brought with her a large black dog which looked like a collie. "Your wife says," stated the medium, "I like the brown dog you have now, but Roy was always my favourite." Mr. Findlay does at present own a brown dog and Roy was the name of the black collie he had for many years.

Sometimes, at séances, evidence is provided which the recipients cannot substantiate until inquiries have been made.

Mrs. G. Vivian said in "Light," the psychic journal, that her "dead" daughter repeatedly insisted at sittings that there were horses in her spirit environment. When this girl was on earth, she had an intense love for horses, and a great understanding of their character.

Through different mediums, the mother was told, "I now have with me a horse B——," followed by the statement, "Chestnut brown horse with a white fore-front I used to ride when I was about ten years."

Although Mrs. Vivian had no personal recollection of a horse of this description she was told by the riding-master her daughter had as a child that the information was accurate. The child frequently rode a horse named Bridget answering to this description. The animal passed over after her daughter "died."

On another occasion when describing a garden in the spirit world her daughter said, "And tell Daddy there are birds here." No doubt the "dead" girl knew her father would be interested in this fact because he had always encouraged his children to take an interest in bird life, a subject which appealed to him.

Still another proof was provided by the spirit girl when she informed her mother that she had with her a dog who used to belong to one of her school friends. The dog's name, Jock, and description of the animal were supplied, as well as the location of the house in which he had lived.

Mrs. Vivian had no personal knowledge of the dog whose name her "dead" daughter had said was Jock and it was not until a year later that she met the dog's owner who confirmed the spirit statements.

CHAPTER XIII

THEY ALL COME BACK

MRS. FLORENCE KINGSTONE, besides being a great lover of animals, is also a very fine medium. At the Stead Bureau, founded by W. T. Stead, the famous journalist and social reformer, she once held a series of séances which were confined only to clairvoyant descriptions of animals.

Because so many people were anxious to know about their pets who had passed on, the medium would only concentrate on the "dead" animals whom she saw, in order that she might give comfort to their human friends..

On one occasion, Mrs. Kingston saw many spirit forms of animals surrounding one of the sitters. She could not understand the reason for such an assembly of pets, until the woman explained that she was a veterinary surgeon!

She told the medium that her own special pet was among the group of animals that had been described. Mrs. Kingstone not only singled out this favourite dog from the rest, but supplied further evidence by recalling the fact that this animal had met its "death" through being accidentally shot in the neck by a gamekeeper.

At another of these special "animal circles," Mrs. Kingstone saw the spirit forms of two dachshunds. She described them to one of the sitters. She told the woman that she saw with these two dogs a kind of large wicker basket which appeared to have an oilskin cover. It seemed to be a sort of kennel, but was different from any she had seen before.

"Oh," said the woman, "I understand perfectly. You have described the special wicker basket I had made for the two dogs in which they travelled three times to South Africa and back."

On one occasion, when a woman called for a private sitting, Mrs. Kingstone saw clairvoyantly the spirit body of a dog which entered the room almost simultaneously with the caller. "Are you worried about your dog?" the medium asked her. The young woman merely shrugged her shoulders and would not reply.

The medium went into trance. Not until the sitting came to an end, and the medium returned to her normal condition, did the sitter tell her that she had received satisfactory evidence about her dog. She said that the guide had described him correctly and told her that he had only passed on that week.

Mrs. Kingstone once had a psychic experience which she finds difficult to explain. Whether she witnessed an incident that had not yet taken place in the cycle of time, or whether the experience was given to her as a warning of the dog's impending "death," is a matter for conjecture.

She left her Pomeranian dog Vic in one room. While going into another part of the house, the medium saw the animal's etherealised form floating in the air before her eyes. Anxious to know whether Vic was all right, she returned to the room in which she had left him. The little Pom greeted her in his accustomed manner, and appeared to be in his usual good health.

But, four days afterwards, the dog "died" after a sudden heart seizure.

Not long ago, Mrs. Kingstone received a letter from an unknown woman living in Blackburn. This correspondent told her she had read an article in "Psychic News" on her descriptions of "dead" animals.

"I have suffered deep distress over the loss of a dog," she wrote. "Though it is nearly a year ago, my trouble seems scarcely to abate. I am wondering if you would give me any consolation or assurance of his existence. Sometimes I have thought he is with me, but this may be only imagination... Perhaps I ought to explain that I know very little about Spiritualism... I do so desperately crave my dog."

Never being able to turn a deaf ear to the plea of one in distress over an animal, Mrs. Kingstone concentrated on the woman's letter. Soon, her clairvoyant powers began to function, and she saw the spirit form of a blue-eyed, bearded man. He indicated that his name was William, and gave the time of his passing.

He brought with him a dog with a bandaged paw. The medium could not catch the animal's name other than that it began with the letter "R."

She wrote to the woman in Blackburn, telling her what she had experienced, and received a delighted acknowledgment. William was the name of the woman's father whose appearance, as well as the time of his passing, had been correctly given. The dog's name was Rex and, while on earth, his paw was frequently bandaged because he was a chronic sufferer from blisters between his toes.

Thus, one more grief-stricken human was comforted with the assurance that her dog still survived—by someone she had never even seen.

Cat and dog friendships are common enough, but I do not imagine many people have made a pet of a cow!

For some years Mrs. Elizabeth Sillman lived on an Australian farm where she and her children made a great pet of a very ancient cow named Darkie. Because she reciprocated the love they had for her, the cow would let the little ones climb all over her and, in fact, take any liberty they liked.

From a farmer's point of view, Darkie was quite worthless, and when cattle feed was scarce, her fate would often hang in the balance. But the children would set up such howls of distress at the possibility of losing their good-natured friend, that they would get their way in the end. Darkie continued to be their good-tempered companion.

In addition to the cow, there was also a neighbour's dog who took a great fancy to this family of animal lovers. Spot, a white dog with a black patch, used to spend as much time as possible with his adopted family. In fact, when his rightful owners moved from the neighbourhood to a town fifty-five miles away, he walked the whole way back to the farmhouse in the burning heat! They found him on the doorstep one morning, footsore and famished for want of food.

The time came when Mrs. Sillman had to leave Australia and travel to England with her family. Because there was no alternative, Darkie had to be turned over to other hands for destruction—she would not have been a paying proposition to any farmer—and Spot, the dog, had to be returned to his own home.

Over a year later, Mrs. Sillman visited a Spiritualist church in England. At that time, she was a stranger to the district. Nobody even knew her name. Nevertheless, at this meeting, the medium who was giving clairvoyance described Darkie to the astonished visitor, and gave details of the animal's characteristics and habits. Moreover, she went on to describe a white dog with a dark patch who, she said, was trying to attract attention.

Mrs. Sillman's mind went back to all the dogs who had belonged to her. The medium's description did not fit any of them, and so she had to say she had never owned such an animal.

It did not strike her at the time that it might be a dog who had decided to "own" her. For so it transpired! In her next mail from Australia was a letter to say that Spot had been run over and killed. The date of the medium's accurate description of the white dog with the black patch coincided with the time Spot had been killed.

He had once walked fifty-five miles in order to return to the ones he loved better than his rightful owners. This time, he had made a different journey. He came back from the other side of life to greet the woman who had always shown him kindness. Spot may not have belonged to her in the strict sense of ownership, but the love of a little dog pays no heed to such trifles.

Another dog who did not really belong to the one to whom he returned was known as Old Bob. He had, in his lifetime been helped, under difficult circumstances, by Miss K. Doming. She found him outside their home one day, and befriended him until he was eventually returned to his rightful owners. He passed on a short time afterwards.

Some time later, she attended a Spiritualist meeting where the medium said to her, "There is a large, brown shaggy dog with you. He is looking into your face with love and gratitude in his eyes."

Miss Doming said she could not recognise the description. She had never owned a dog of this kind. But when the medium went on to say that the dog was known as Old Bob, she remembered the animal she had befriended.

Evidently, Old Bob, whom the medium accurately described, had returned to show his gratitude for her past kindness to him.

Occasionally, when it appears that a medium has given an inaccurate or inadequate description of a spirit, it often transpires that the memory of the person addressed is at fault. It is not always easy to remember events that have happened in the distant past. Afterwards, when these people have had time to think over what the clairvoyant had said, they recall certain things that prove the description was right after all.

A medium once described a black and white spaniel who had suffered from paralysis when on earth. The woman to whom she gave this message had recently had a dog "put to sleep" because a motor accident left the dog in an intensely nervous condition. She told the medium that she must have mistaken the breed, as the animal was a Lakeland terrier, and its coat had been black and fawn before the accident.

When the woman returned home she recalled that, thirty years ago, she *did* have *a black and white spaniel* who had to be "put to sleep" because it developed *paralysis.*

Striking evidence of her dog's survival was given to Mrs. Margaret A. Tucker, by Mr. Jack McKay, an Edinburgh medium.

He told her he could see a dog with her. "I've seen the kind often," he said, "but can't name it as I know nothing about dogs. It is longer than it is high, is black and *white* in colour although you probably wouldn't call it that. He has one of his fore-legs heavily bandaged, and has a great swathing of bandages criss-crossed over here—" passing his hand over his chest and shoulders. "What a love that dog brings you!" he declared.

Mrs. Tucker told "Psychic News" that fully nine years before his passing, the dog, a beautiful black and *silver* spaniel, fell into a deep hole in the nearby woods and broke a fore-leg in two places and also his shoulder.

In order to allow time for the swellings to subside, the animal was drugged for some hours before the veterinary surgeon would attempt to set the fractures. Then, she acted as anaesthetist to him while he did his work. Later on, the vet stood by while she removed the splints.

When the dog saw his leg once again, he whimpered with delight and held it out to Mrs. Tucker to see. "How that dog loves you!" commented the vet.

Almost the self-same words were used by the medium when he described the dog who had returned from the Other Side to prove that love, as well as life, continues after the body has perished.

Not only were the colour and markings of Mrs. Maud Coles's "dead" dog accurately described to her at a public meeting, but the medium's message greatly comforted the owner and impressed, by its accuracy, her husband, who had doubts about the truth of Spiritualism.

The medium correctly described the "dead" animal as "a little black and white dog, with two black spots on its back, and a black-and-tan face." She went on to say that the animal was barking delightedly, and was pulling her frock in an effort to drag the medium towards the owner. "The dog is showing me how happy she is to be free from pain," said the medium.

That message made Mrs. Coles very happy, for the dog had suffered much before passing. "When I told my doubting husband about the message, he was astonished and thought that it was wonderful," she said.

Perhaps because he is so devoted to animals, Mr. Harold Sharp is able to say, "In my own mediumship I have seen quite as many animals manifest as human beings."

He had, for several years, a blue Mangaby monkey to whom he was very attached. Now that the animal has passed on, he still comes back to pay an occasional visit to his owner. The monkey still displays his earthly characteristics, his vanity and his liking for admiration. Whenever a medium is giving clairvoyance to Mr. Sharp—for psychics usually like to get evidence independently of their own gifts—the monkey is not happy until he is described.

Soon after the animal "died," he made his return known. His spirit form appeared in the séance room, where he proceeded to jump from chair to chair. Two cushions were flung to the floor and a picture fell from the wall before he was satisfied that he had made sufficient upheaval to assure his owner he was still the same mischievous, vain, but lovable pet.

Several mediums have described Mr. Harold Sharp's "dead" mother, who has been able to provide proof, not only of her own survival, but of her beloved animals now with her in the spirit world. When he sat with Mrs. E. M. Neville, she said, "I see a great, overshadowing tree with a child's swing suspended from the branches. There is a woman beneath the tree. She is crocheting while seated in a wicker chair. How she must have loved animals! There are two dogs with her—no three—and lots of cats. A lamb and—no, it can't be—yes, it is—a pig! It seems to be a most intelligent animal as it runs grunting towards me."

The medium's psychic vision had enabled her to describe the surroundings of Mr. Sharp's old home. "How often," he says, "my mother would take her needlework to sit beneath the old walnut tree in the orchard, while, sitting on the swing, I would read aloud to her.

"For several years we had a tame pig. It became quite a member of the family. It had been hurt at birth. My mother took it from its noisy, pushing, greedy litter, and gave it a hay-lined box in the kitchen, where she fed it regularly from a baby's feeding bottle. It grew to adore my mother and would run around the village after her, grunting by her side like a regular old gossip. At the time when farmers usually send their pigs to the butcher we none of us had the heart to let Wiggie go. She remained the pet of the family for several years."

Not only had the medium described the other animals who used to surround his mother, but she proved that the rather unusual pet of the family still lived.

"My mother was such a born animal lover," says Mr. Sharp, "that wherever she went everyone's animals went to her as to a magnet."

On many occasions, different mediums have told him that his mother now works on the animal plane, especially amongst those creatures who have been slaughtered. She helps to soothe and calm them in the state of bewildered terror to which they awaken on being suddenly flung into another existence.

Mr. Sharp's mediumistic gifts once enabled him to ease a woman's morbid fears that she had not fulfilled her duty to her "dead" mother in regard to her pet. Rendered sleepless with anxiety, the woman decided that she might get some help by sitting with a medium.

While he was in trance, Mr. Sharp's guide described a spirit whom she recognised as her mother. Then, the guide told her, "She is so grateful to you for sending Tips to her."

Now before her mother passed on, the daughter had promised her that she would always look after her beloved cat, Tips. Unfortunately, soon after her mother's "death," the cat became seriously ill. Unable to ease the animal's suffering, the vet said the most merciful thing to do would be to have Tips "put to sleep." To this she agreed, but afterwards became consumed with fear that she had betrayed her promise to her mother to cherish the animal. The "dead" woman's words not only put her mind at rest, but gave her the additional comfort of knowing that the cat was still alive and with her mother once again.

When Mr. Harold Sharp visited Russia, he became acquainted with a young electrical engineer who was very mediumistic. Accompanied by his friend's big, yellow dog, the two men often explored the countryside. One day, after a long cycle ride, they rested under some trees. Suddenly, Mr. Sharp noticed another dog playing happily with his friend's animal. As they were some miles away from any habitation, he was astonished at its sudden appearance. "Where has that dog sprung from?" he asked his companion.

The man appeared to notice the newcomer for the first time. He looked again, as though unable to believe his own eyes and, in a questioning kind of voice, called the animal towards him.

The strange dog bounded forward in evident delight. "But as my friend commenced to pat it," says Mr. Sharp, "the dog completely and instantly vanished!"

Afterwards, when he had got over his surprise, the man told him that the sire of his present dog had been run over and killed two years previously. No wonder he was astonished at the sight and the touch of this "dead" dog who appeared from nowhere and vanished so suddenly!

"I am still wondering," says Mr. Sharp, "if this was a case of actual materialisation, or if two sympathetic mediums had 'tuned-in' objectively to the same vibration."

Mr. Harold Sharp told me a moving story about Dandy, a dear old black and grey dog who was owned by Mr. and Mrs. W. Baldwin. Dandy was a highly privileged member of the family. Perhaps the member of the household who adored him most of all was Annie, the maidservant. At nine o'clock every night, Dandy would rouse himself from his place in the living room and make his way to the kitchen where Annie would have his supper ready for him.

But he knew when Annie's free evenings came round. On these days, he would, of his own accord, go into the kitchen and bring his empty enamel plate into the living-room to remind his owners that it was *their* turn to feed him!

Of course, Dandy's self-taught "performance" with his empty plate was duly appreciated and applauded by visitors to the Baldwins' house, and the dog thoroughly enjoyed basking in the limelight of their admiration.

As the years passed, he became old, faltering, and nearly blind. But, because he knew every inch of the familiar house and garden, he still enjoyed life and the love that all his human friends showered upon his wise and ancient head.

Mr. Baldwin became ill. His doctor advised him to leave London and return north to breathe his native air. Simultaneously with this medical dictum, the old dog's sight became even worse. The vet advised his being "put to sleep."

Realising that an ailing, old, blind dog would be unhappy torn from his familiar surroundings, Dandy's owners were reluctantly forced to agree with this recommendation. Nevertheless, they found it hard to make the final arrangements for parting with their dear old four-legged friend.

Annie, the maid, had, in the meantime, found a new post, but regularly called to see her former employers—and her beloved Dandy.

The day for Mr. and Mrs. Baldwin's departure northwards drew very near. Mrs. Baldwin said to her husband, "You really must go to the vet today and make arrangements for poor old Dandy to be put to sleep." Her husband answered that as Annie would be calling that day, and would want to say good-bye to Dandy, he would wait until the following morning.

That afternoon Annie called. She took Dandy for his favourite walk. Then she put him safely into his basket and bade him an affectionate farewell. She told her late employers, in the living room, that the dog had seemed very happy in her company that day. She lingered, talking about her new post. Then, prior to leaving the house, she quietly opened the kitchen door and whispered a last "Good night" to the sleeping dog.

Later, Mr. Baldwin opened the kitchen door and called to Dandy with the intention of taking him for his usual bed-time walk. But there was no response from the dog. Dandy lay in his basket, silent and still. Looking at the quiet, lifeless body, Mr. Baldwin saw that the vet's services were now unnecessary. The hand of nature had put Dandy's physical body to sleep!

The following evening Mr. Harold Sharp visited Mr. and Mrs. Baldwin. For certain domestic reasons they did not tell the medium of the dog's passing. They were all talking together in the living room when, at nine o'clock, the door suddenly swung open. Mr. Sharp turned his head and said casually, "Hello, Dandy!"

For there, enamel plate in mouth, stood Dandy, waiting in the old familiar manner for the accustomed burst of approbation which always greeted his performance.

So clearly had Dandy manifested that the medium, unaware of his passing, mistook the dog's spirit body for his earthly presence.

Later, when the medium was entranced, his guide spoke of Dandy's passing to the spirit world. He said that when Annie had opened the kitchen door to whisper a last good-bye to the dog, his spirit was already free, and had bounded happily towards her, and accompanied his faithful human friend part of the way home.

There had always been a strong bond of affection between Mr. Harold Sharp and Dandy. It is not surprising, therefore, that the "dead" dog frequently shows himself clearly and distinctly to this medium who affirms, "Dandy still lives, free from the limitations from which he was so happily liberated."

CHAPTER XIV

PROOFS BY SPIRIT PHOTOGRAPHY

THE well-known psychic photographer, Mr. William Hope, of Crewe, who has now passed on, took hundreds of pictures on which the "dead" appeared. These spirit "extras" have been recognised by relatives and friends. He worked in collaboration with Mrs. A. Buxton, whose psychic power gave added support to his own remarkable mediumship.

Some members of Mrs. Buxton's family met one day for the express purpose of having a psychic photograph taken by Mr. Hope. Mrs. Buxton's father had recently passed on. They hoped that he would succeed in showing himself as an "extra" if they sat in a group.

The medium took the photograph, but instead of the expected relative there appeared on the plate an "extra" of a terrier. The delight of Mrs. Buxton in recognising her "dead" pet Floss somewhat made up for the disappointment of the absence of her father's picture.

A curious thing about the spirit form of the dog is that it appears on the lap of Mrs. Buxton's sister Amy. Amy, unfortunately, was unable to control her antipathy towards animals. No doubt for a reason beyond her own will, she could not bear to be in the room with them. In consequence whenever she paid Mrs. Buxton a visit, poor Floss had to be removed to another part of the house.

I do not know why Floss appeared on Amy's lap in the photograph. Perhaps the terrier wanted to impress on the sitter that she bore her no ill will for the number of times she caused Floss to be removed from the living-room when she visited the Buxtons' house! At any rate, the psychic picture is a clear and distinct likeness of the terrier.

A woman who visited Mr. Hope to try to get a photograph of a "dead" relative was amazed to find the "extra" of a cat when the plate was developed.

The cat, a great pet of the family, "died" only a week before the sitting. The psychic photograph on which the cat manifested itself is most interesting. In addition to the "extra" of the animal there appear the words, "Dear parents," written by the sitter's child who was in the spirit world. The woman was psychically informed that her child was looking after the cat who had so recently passed on. A long written communication, in clear but minute writing from those on the Other Side, makes the psychic photograph a unique one.

"Psychic Science" records how, one day, Mr. Hope took a picture of Mr. and Mrs. Buxton on the steps of a caravan on the seashore at Exmouth. When the plate was developed, it showed two "extras." One was the "dead" son of the Buxtons. The other was of a pony named Tommy, who passed on before their son. The two had been great friends when on earth.

The psychic photograph is reproduced in "Psychic Science." A picture of Tommy, taken before he "died," also appears for comparison with the spirit picture of the same animal.

Mrs. A. E. Deane used to take psychic photographs at the Stead Bureau. Mrs. Garling Drury and a woman friend decided to have a joint sitting with this medium. When one plate was developed, there appeared the "extra" of Mrs. Drury's pet dog who had recently passed on. Although the psychic picture of the animal is not clear enough for reproduction, I have myself been able to identify it by comparing it with a picture taken before it "died." Mrs. Drury's friend was also made happy by the sitting for, on the same photograph, her "dead" mother was able to impinge her likeness.

In addition to professional psychic photographers, sometimes ordinary people discover that they have taken pictures which show "extras." Often, they have had no idea that they possessed this form of mediumship. When Mrs. Filson, using a film camera, took a snapshot of Lady Hehir and her Irish wolf-hound, Tara, she never expected any supernormal results. When, however, the film was developed, one of the snaps showed an "extra" of Kathal, a cairn puppy whose short life had been spent in the keeping of Lady Hehir. He "died" in her arms.

Major T. R. Morse, who sent notes of the case to the British College of Psychic Science, said that the cairn and the wolf-hound had been inseparable friends. He writes, "The puppy was in the habit of lying by the big dog in the position shown by the photograph, although the wolf-hound is standing instead of lying down in the picture. The kennelman and others at once recognised the puppy without any clue being given. Lady Hehir had an enlargement of the photograph made which shows the details more clearly, and with a magnifying glass the nostrils, feathers on the ears, and every detail is clear."

Another interesting thing about the psychic photograph is that the line of the wolf-hound's back is straighter than it is in reality. This is not caused by any illusion of light and shade or background.

Lady Hehir states in "Psychic Science" that a new film was put into the camera for the occasion by Mrs. Filson, who took four snapshots. All the other pictures came out normally and showed the usual dip in Tara's back.

When the cairn puppy was on earth, the two animals used to eat, play and walk together. Lady Hehir writes, "The spot on the cliffs at which the photo was taken was a favourite spot of theirs, where much of their play together took place on summer evenings. The puppy was always a character, and we all worshipped him."

The psychic picture of the wolf-hound, which clearly shows the "extra" of the cairn puppy, is reproduced in this book. It originally appeared in "Psychic Science," which points out that, apart from the obvious good faith of the witnesses, the photograph, being taken on a film, renders double exposure almost impossible. The film was examined and shows no trace of double exposure on the print.

It is also pointed out that there seems to be nothing in the background that could lend itself to an imaginary resemblance and the photograph was taken in full sunlight, as could be seen by the shadows.

In addition to the psychic picture showing the cairn puppy and the abnormally straight back of the wolf-hound two other pictures are reproduced in "Psychic Science" for comparative purposes. One shows Tara's normally curved back. The other is a photograph of Lady Hehir holding the cairn puppy in her arms. The earthly likeness of the little dog can easily be identified with the spirit photograph of the same animal.

I do not know the explanation of Tara's abnormally straight back seen in the psychic picture. Possibly, the thickening is caused by ectoplasm, the substance used to "build up" the spirit forms. In most spirit pictures, ectoplasm can clearly be seen surrounding the extras.

In speaking of her affection for the "dead" puppy, Lady Hehir says, "I feel convinced that he is often in the room with Tara and me, as she talks in a soft, crooning way to something she, evidently sees.

Mrs. T. W. Moore owned a white mongrel terrier with dark head markings. During his earthly life he had a favourite spot in the garden. Stretched in his particular corner, just outside the living room door which opened direct on to the garden, Chris would lie for hours at a time.

A few months after the dog passed on, Mrs. Moore took some snapshots of different parts of her garden. When the films were developed, there was an "extra" on the snapshot which showed the living-room door. It was Chris, lying in his old accustomed corner of the garden.

The spirit picture is not sharp enough for reproduction in this book, but I have examined and compared it, to my satisfaction, with a picture of Chris taken before his "death." The same dark markings on the dog's head can be seen in both photographs.

CHAPTER XV

OUTSIDE THE SÉANCE ROOM

IT is not only at séances and Spiritualist meetings that "dead" animals have manifested their presence.

Mrs. Gladys Osborne Leonard has had several experiences of their survival through her own remarkable mediumistic powers.

In her book, "The Last Crossing," she relates how her "dead" dog was brought to see her by her husband in the spirit world.

She writes, "For many years my husband and I owned a very intelligent, domineering, autocratic, disobedient, belligerent, and withal lovable Pekingese. Doesn't this description fit the majority of the breed? Eleven years ago she died at the age of fourteen. My husband was profoundly attached to this dog, whom we had called Ching, regardless of the fact that it was a female.

"A few weeks ago I was awakened from a sound sleep by feeling something moving about on my bed, close to my right shoulder. I was lying on my left side, a little on my face. Whatever it was on the bed was patting or pawing my shoulder. I was rather startled for a moment, as the touch was so `solid' and definite.

"Remembering that nothing evil could touch me so long as I myself realised the paramount power of good, I pulled myself together, and tried to put my left hand and arm (on which I had been partly lying) out from under the bedclothes, and to reach back over my right shoulder in an endeavour to touch whatever it was that was touching me. In doing this I found, as had happened before in such cases, that I was partly cataleptic.

"The room was not quite dark; I could see the fireplace, mantelpiece, and cupboard door opposite me.

"Making a tremendous mental effort, I managed to extend my hand out and back over my shoulder. Anybody who has had a similar experience will understand how difficult a feat it is to move about at all during the cataleptic condition. If it is very deep, it is impossible to move at all for the time being, but even if one is only partly so, it feels as if the limbs are weighted with lead' when we attempt to move them. However, I succeeded, and my hand came into contact with a fluffy, furry object."

Because of her cataleptic state, the medium found it a great struggle to move or to speak. Nevertheless, she managed to ask, "Is it Ching?" before she sank into a still deeper condition of catalepsy.

"As this was happening," continues Mrs. Leonard, "I became conscious that my etheric body was moving slightly out from my physical, and I realised that my consciousness was beginning to operate in both bodies simultaneously.

"A curious feature of these circumstances is that one seems *to* see the etheric objects with about the same-or only slightly more-clarity than that with which one sees the physical... The darkness of the room appears to affect the etheric vision to about the same extent as it does the physical.

"This, I think, may be entirely due to the cataleptic condition which limits the faculty of sight in the etheric body while it is *so* closely associated with the physical counterpart. As one is seeing in both bodies simultaneously, it may well be that the amount of consciousness of seeing is halved. As I say, this is usually more noticeable when the subject is in a state of entire or partial catalepsy, which I have found customary when power is being taken from us by the etheric operators in order to produce some definite manifestation on the physical plane.

"As soon as I became aware that my faculty of sight was operating in my etheric body, and that I could see and feel *without moving my physical body,* I gave up all effort, and prepared myself to observe carefully anything that might happen."

At the foot of the bed, the medium then saw the spirit form of her "dead" husband. He was looking, with a great deal of interest at the antics of the moving object on her bed. She was able to put out her etheric arm. She touched the furry form on her bed, and immediately identified it as the body of Ching, her little Pekingese.

Mrs. Leonard writes, "I passed my etheric hand over head, back, and under her chest. When she realised that I was doing so, she nearly went mad with delight. She plunged, and leapt, and rolled over. As she rolled on my hand, I felt that she weighed about the same as she had in her earthly life. The soft silky hair on her chest, and the long hanging ears were the same. I remembered how, long ago, she used to plunge about and roll over on my hand while I was trying to stroke her when I awoke in the mornings, and she knew that at last the time had arrived when I would speak to her and touch her again after the long night's silence.

"During this time I could see both my husband and the dog, and though the light from the window was dim, I noticed there was a kind of faint, luminous glow in the vicinity of my husband's body, and that of the dog. As I fondled her, my husband answered the question I had asked when I first tried to touch her, saying, 'Yes, it is Ching,' as if he was afraid I should doubt the evidence of my own senses unless he assured me that it was really so.

In concluding the description of her experience, Mrs. Leonard writes of the happy emotion that followed this psychic manifestation: "As always, after such an experience, I felt comforted and soothed." When they had gone, she mentally asked a blessing on her husband and the little dog. Then, having rendered thanks for the joy their visit had brought her, the medium fell into a deep, restful sleep.

Often animals have been clairvoyantly seen when there have been no apparent psychic surroundings, and sometimes a visitor has thought that the animal was actually an earthly member of the household.

I have collected some of these stories.

A woman, whose husband is a solicitor, described his experience in "Psychic News." "He had no knowledge of Spiritualism," she said, "and had never read or studied the subject. Indeed, he was considerably prejudiced against what he called 'meddling with these things.'"

One day, he had to go to a country house to visit a woman. She was a new client and her house was completely strange to him. On his return he told his wife of a delightful dog who ran in front of his client and kept stopping and looking up in her face. "I don't know when I have seen a dog with such a beautiful head or one that looked so devoted," he said.

Later, when her husband's client took a flat in London, they both visited her. During tea the solicitor asked his hostess, "What have you done with your dog?" There was an awkward silence for a moment before she answered abruptly, "I have no dog."

When the solicitor had gone into another room, his client told his wife apologetically, "I suppose I am a fool over dogs, but I had such a terrible experience with one I loved—more than anything in the world that I'll never have another. When war came, I went to France to drive a lorry and left my dog at home with my father and mother. They got fed up with the country, closed the house, and went up to their town house, leaving my dog in the care of a stableman who starved and ill-treated it. I got back only in time for it to die on my lap."

"What sort of a dog was it?" asked her guest.

"A white Highland terrier," she replied.

The solicitor and his wife left. As soon as they were outside the house he exclaimed, "It's a rum thing about that dog. I'll swear I saw a dog there."

"What sort of dog did you see?" his wife asked.

"A white Highland terrier," he answered.

Miss Isabel Wood told in "The Cat" of her psychic experience concerning a much loved yellow cat. This animal, a great pet of the family, disappeared from home one day. All efforts to trace him failed, and although he knew his way about the neighbourhood perfectly, he never returned. Greater than their sorrow in losing him was the anguish of not knowing what had happened to him.

About three weeks after his disappearance, the whole household was awakened in the early hours of the morning by a loud double knocking at the hall door. Miss Wood went downstairs to see who could be calling at the house at such an early hour. She opened the front door, but there was nobody to be seen. "But," she said, "as I glanced down before shutting the door, I saw the shadowy form of a yellow cat enter, cross the hall and disappear at the front of the stairs. I made no more heartbreaking journeys in search of our lost pet."

The Rev. Charles L. Tweedale, Vicar of Weston, Yorkshire, described his experiences of animal survival in a local paper in response to a question on the subject.

"As a result of a unique psychic experience," he said, "I am in a position to answer the question unhesitatingly in the affirmative, and to testify that some animals—especially those that have been closely associated with man—undoubtedly *do* survive!"

The Rev. Charles Tweedale said that one of his relatives had a dog to whom she was very much attached. This dog "died," and five years later, his owner also passed on.

Five years after her passing she began to be seen in broad daylight. Sometimes, several people would see her at the same time. Her dog—was also seen with her, every spot and characteristic being accurately shown. Even the trembling eagerness the dog had displayed in earthly life continued to manifest in the spirit body of the animal. The thinness of hair which allowed the skin to show through could also be seen in the spirit form.

"On one occasion," wrote the vicar, "when my mother endeavoured to embrace the apparition of her sister, the dog growled, as though defending its mistress. On another occasion my little daughter, then only eight months old, followed it upstairs accompanied by several other persons, and when it disappeared under an article of furniture she crawled after it, calling for the doggie."

Another child, little more than a baby, has also seen the form of a dog who had passed over. The child's mother, Mrs. Goddard, described the incident in "Dog World," a Bradford paper. She wrote:

"I have had a few cocker spaniels for a great number of years now. At one time they used to run all over the house as they chose, but when my daughter was practically still only a baby I found that she was apt to give them any food that she was given herself I never knew how much the dogs had had, and how much the daughter! So we had to make a strict rule that they were not allowed in the dining-room at meal times.

"A time came when my oldest and best beloved dog, Jill, had to be put to sleep. I locked all the other dogs in their kennels. The veterinary surgeon came at 11 a.m. and later buried her for me in the garden. I left the dogs shut up and said nothing to the child, who was then about two-and-a-half years old. At luncheon we were sitting together in the dining-room, she in her high chair beside me, when she looked down at a space on the carpet between us and said: 'Oh, Mummy, there's Jill.' She was surprised a dog should be in the dining room at the forbidden hour. I said, 'No darling.' The child looked over the arm of her chair again and said, 'Is it Tess? No, Mummy, it is Jill.'

"Tess was Jill's daughter and like her in colouring, but the child knew them apart as well as I did. In any case, Tess was in the kennel with the others. I made no comment and the child took no further notice, and went on with her luncheon."

Mrs. Florence Kingstone is not the only clairvoyant member of her family. When her daughter was only three years old, the child saw the spirit form of their cat Tookie, whose recent passing had been carefully concealed from her. Tookie was a great pet of the. family. His favourite seat was the top of the dining table, on one particular corner.

When the cat reached the age of eighteen, life began to be somewhat of a burden to him. Mrs. Kingstone regretfully came to the conclusion that it would be kind to have him put painlessly to sleep. An appointment was made for the vet to come to the house to assist Tookie's passing, and for the worn body to be taken away when the animal had gone to sleep.

As her little girl was very attached to Tookie, her mother did not want to distress her by seeing these arrangements carried out. Mrs. Kingstone therefore sent the little girl away from home before the vet called. Strangely enough, the child made no comment whatever on the animal's disappearance when she returned home. She did not refer to the fact in any way until three days later.

Then, that morning, the child pointed to the cat's favourite corner of the dining table and exclaimed, "Look, Mummy, there's Tookie, there's Tookie!"

"The greatest joy and comfort of my life is to know that, when my call comes, my four-footed friends will be waiting to welcome me," writes a woman who has clairvoyantly seen her animals after they have passed on.

One night, she was sitting nursing a sick Airedale, when the spirit form of another dog of the same breed who passed on four years previously appeared in the room. This psychic vision gave her the impression that the sick dog would soon join the other one. When on earth, the animals had been very attracted to each other. The woman's impression was justified, for the following day the sick dog passed over.

"One of my dogs always sat in an armchair with me," continues the writer. "He loved to try to push me off the chair when I played with him. Some months after he 'died' my mother was sitting in the same armchair and was suddenly pushed from the chair for no apparent reason."

There was a dog in the room who had been the constant companion of the one who had passed over. This dog, who had ceaselessly fretted for his lost friend, looked up at the armchair, barked and wagged his tail in great delight. He could, apparently, see the spirit form of the "dead" dog who was manifesting his presence by playing one of his old familiar games on the chair. His delight lasted only as long as he saw his companion's spirit form. As it disappeared, the earthly dog lay down and cried piteously.

The lonely animal continued to fret for the other one until, a few months later, he too passed to the Other Side.

Can there be any doubt that the two affectionate friends have resumed their old companionship? I think not!

Two days after Bengy, a wire-haired terrier, passed on, his owner told a woman friend what had occurred. "Oh, I wish I had been able to say good-bye to him before he went," said her friend, who was very attached to the dog.

Did Bengy hear her expression of regret?

That same night, she was awakened by the touch of a dog's paws. She also felt the materialised animal licking her face. He was obviously delighted when she acknowledged him as Bengy, and showed that she understood he had come to bid her the belated good-bye.

The following instance of animal survival was given by Charles J. Seymour to "Psychic News": "At a developing circle a sitter stated that she had clairvoyantly seen a cat walking to and fro. That night I had some writing to do, and turned into bed to complete it.

"I was about to switch off the light, when I heard the unmistakable mewing of a cat. It lasted from eight to ten seconds. I could locate exactly the spot whence the sound appeared to issue-the centre of a bedside rug-but, though I had my gaze fixed on it from the first moment, I could see nothing.

"We have no cat, but—to anticipate the sceptics—I made a careful search not only of the room but of the whole house (my family were away at the time and I was alone in it) for a possible stray. There was no cat.

"A few days later, I asked the control of a different medium, 'Can you tell me anything about a cat?' The reply was: 'Yes, it was your cat, a black cat, and it has been on the Other Side rather a long time.'

"Our black cat, Timmie, 'died' over ten years ago. We were so attached to him, and he to us, that we have not cared to replace him. Indeed, he showed a very unusual degree of affection. On one occasion when we were all away from home for some months and left him with a friend, he went almost crazy with delight on seeing us return."

Two days after Mr. Sydney Lockwood's mother left her home to spend a holiday in Devonshire, he found her much loved cat "dead" on her bed.

Not wishing to spoil his mother's holiday, he did not write and tell his mother what had happened. But the first words she said to her son on her return were, "You need not tell me about my cat. It materialised to me in the fields of Devonshire. I know it is 'dead.'"

Mrs. Osborne Leonard's secretary, Mr. Walter Wilson, wrote to me about his own psychic experiences which followed the "death" of his dog.

Mr. Wilson has a habit of sitting with his elbows on his knees, with his hands hanging loosely clasped. When his dog Philip was on earth, he would often thrust his face between his owner's hands as much as to say, "Don't sit there doing nothing—come out for a walk."

"I have no pretensions to being particularly psychic," Mr. Wilson said, "but many a time, when I have unconsciously fallen into this position, I have distinctly felt Philip's head push my hands apart in the old familiar way."

Once, when he was ill in hospital, his wife was obliged to move into another house. She had left old friends behind in the house she had just vacated. Alone on the first day in her new home, she felt rather forlorn. That night, somewhat sad at heart, she was just settling down to sleep, when she felt something move on the bed.

For a moment she wondered, fearfully, whether it could be a stray cat, or, horrible thought, even a rat! But to her joy, the movement on the bed became the familiar antics their dog used to make when he was on earth. She felt the materialised form turn round two or three times. Then he snuggled comfortably against her back. Philip had made a brief return to assure her that she was not completely alone!

In "Psychic Science" appears the story of a young man who, staying with his friend's parents, was disturbed in his sleep by a cat jumping on his bed and sitting on his chest.

Being very fond of animals, he merely moved the animal off his chest, but still felt it moving under the coverlet where he left her before he went to sleep. But, when he told the family of the incident, they were greatly astonished.

Their only cat had, on account of illness, recently been "put to sleep." The animal had been a great pet of the member of the family whose bed the visitor had occupied the previous night.

Although the young man knew nothing of these facts, it seems that the "dead" cat had sensed that he too was an animal lover and would not mind being disturbed by the pet who had been in the habit of sleeping on that bed.

Four days after he had passed over, Mrs. Maude Southwell's cat Billikins returned to show his beloved owner that her faith in his survival was justified. She had nursed the sick cat for several days and, just when he was breathing his last she said, "Oh, Billikins, I shall miss you so. Come back if you can."

Four mornings afterwards there was a thud on the bedclothes, and she heard the sound of purring. The cat was greeting his mistress in the old way, for it had been his habit to inform her in this manner that it was time to get up. Mrs. Southwell's husband also heard the "dead" cat purr quite distinctly.

Some time later, Mrs. Southwell acquired a kitten. Unfortunately this second pet became ill and lay dying by the side of his distressed owner. Heartbroken at being unable to relieve the kitten's suffering, she sent out a mental call that he might be helped to pass over peacefully.

She says, "Immediately I felt Billikins's soft fur brush against my hand." At the same time, the dying kitten gave a little sigh, stretched his body—and lay quiet.

The sound of her first cat's purring could be heard so distinctly that a friend of Mrs. Southwell who was in the room said, "Where on earth is that cat purring? It can't be the kitten. He's far too ill. It sounds just like Billikins."

But when Mrs. Southwell said that it was indeed the "dead" cat, her friend, who knew little of the facts of Spiritualism, looked at her in a pitying manner as if she thought Mrs. Southwell was too upset to realise what she was saying.

When her friend saw that the suffering kitten had, at the moment of hearing the purring from the "dead" cat, passed over quite peacefully and happily, she was somewhat impressed.

When Mrs. Southwell sent out a mental call for help fo, the suffering kitten, I imagine that the human helpers on the Other Side brought Billikins back to comfort his owner and to assure her that the dying kitten would also be received, and looked after in the same way as her beloved Billikins.

Miss B. M. Weller visited some friends and found that their small dog was very ill. She was not surprised to hear, the following week, that Queenie had passed on.

A little later, her two friends came to see her. Miss Weller, who is clairvoyant, was chatting with them when she saw the "dead" dog licking her owner's face. The animal was full of life and vigour. Miss Weller also saw the spirit form of a man in a white coat with the dog. This man indicated that he was a veterinary surgeon whose name was John. She described what she had just seen psychically to her friends. They were delighted, for they understood the description perfectly. Their son, a veterinary surgeon, is helped from the Other Side by Mr. John who, when he was on earth followed the same profession.

How natural that he would try to comfort the two people by showing that he was looking after their dog!

Mrs. Frances Collier had a smooth-haired terrier who was devoted to her. One day he was killed by a passing motor car.

Mrs. Collier told in the "Daily Mail" how, that same night, she sat weeping by the fire with her husband. Suddenly, they both heard a loud whimper under the chair. Her husband exclaimed, "What in the world is that?" The cat, who was extremely jealous of the dog and would never remain in the same room with him, at once got up and looked at the chair. Then, with her fur bristling, she went out of the room.

"I am convinced," said Mrs. Collier, "that my dog's ghost returned."

Another story of an animal's survival also appeared in the same newspaper which published a series of readers' letters on the subject.

Mr. Sydney Stanley said, "In my home, when I was a boy, we had a cat and two kittens who enjoyed nothing better than a romp together in the evenings. The sounds of their running feet were to be heard in an adjoining room."

Certain reasons necessitated having these pets "put to sleep." That same night, he was with his parents in the living-room adjoining the hall when they suddenly heard the sound of the cats' feet running outside the door.

"We stopped what we were doing," said Mr. Stanley, "and literally gasped in amazement while the sounds went on. We ran out to see whether a window had been left open which might have admitted a stray cat, but we found the windows and doors shut and fastened for the night. No cat could have got in or out.

"Yet we had all heard the loud and familiar sound of those cats' running feet up and down the hall."

CHAPTER XVI

"THE GREEN-EYED MONSTER"

JEALOUSY is a mental state which, not being part of the physical make-up, can survive the loss of the body and continue to manifest in the next world.

Because animals have, in common with human beings, the ability to think, to form conclusions, however biased their reasoning may be, they occasionally exhibit this trait in their character.

Domestic animals sometimes show jealousy of other human beings whom they think, rightly or wrongly, are encroaching on affection that could be given to them. Still more pets have strongly jealous feeling towards any other animals introduced into their own particular environment.

My own cat was made so unhappy through jealousy on the only two occasions I tried to introduce another animal into my home, that I realised I could only keep another pet at the expense of Paddy's contentment. He normally has a sweet disposition where other animals are concerned, so long as he does not think they are going to live in his home permanently.

Cats are curious creatures! Paddy never shows the slightest sign that he is appreciative of all the affection that he gets—he is thoroughly spoilt! But his behaviour indicates that he reasons he might possibly be deprived of the attention he appears to scorn.

Once, for a few weeks, I kept a cat who had lost his own home in rather tragic circumstances. I hoped that Paddy would get used to Nukie, who had a lovable disposition and seemed to like living with us. Most carefully, we all avoided making any fuss of the newcomer when Paddy was near. Nevertheless, my cat was so jealous of him that he refused to eat, and began to get thin and wretched in appearance.

Worried about my own cat's misery and concerned for Nukie, for whom I could not get another home, I did not know what to do.

Paddy decided the question for me. We went to bed one night leaving the two cats settled for sleep as usual. The next morning the newcomer had disappeared, and Paddy, looking decidedly happier, ate with appetite. We had heard no noise in the night, but Paddy must have induced the other cat to leave. Whether by fair means or, as I suspect, foul, I have never discovered. Although I made exhaustive inquiries and searched the neighbourhood, I never found poor little Nukie again. I hope somebody gave him a good home where there were no other jealous animals!

Mrs. N. Lidyard, of Bath, had a pet cat named Lizzie who was so jealous that she would never allow another cat to approach anywhere near her own domain. This cat passed on about twelve years ago. Since then, Mrs. Lidyard has had twenty-two cats and kittens of all sorts and sizes. But not for long! For various reasons they have left her home. Some, it is true, have "died," but others have disappeared completely.

Mrs. Lidyard wonders whether Lizzie's personality still exercises itself sufficiently strongly to drive all her successors away.

Only a few days after Lizzie passed on, she manifested her presence to her owner in a striking way. The animal had been in the habit of sleeping in one of her owner's shop windows on sunny days. With the setting of the sun, she would follow a regular routine. First, she would arise from her recumbent position and shake herself. Then she would patter along the length of the shop counter, jump down and run to her owner.

"After she had been dead a few days," says Mrs. Lidyard, "I was in the shop serving when, quite suddenly, the patter and jump were distinctly heard by some customers and myself. We looked at each other. 'That was Lizzie's jump,' one of them said." On different occasions, over a period of years, similar manifestations have occurred.

Mrs. A. Main said in "Psychic News," "We had a very intelligent cat in my family for eleven years. It 'died,' much to my regret.

Two or three weeks after its 'death,' we removed from the north of England to the south, and I missed the cat very much indeed. After three or four months, I began to feel as though the animal was still with me."

She was very surprised one night to feel the "dead" animal jump on to the bed. Although she did not see him, she took his materialised paw and shook it as she used to do when the cat was on earth. On one or two mornings, when wide awake, she has seen the cat looking up at her from the side of the bed.

"Once," said Mrs. Main, "I woke and distinctly felt something fade away off the pillow. I heard it purring, at another time. I mentioned the cat's name and was answered by a loud mew. In all, I have had four or five visits from him."

Once, when she was at a Spiritualist church, a medium described the "dead" cat whom she clairvoyantly saw sitting on Mrs. Main's lap.

When Mrs. Mary Bagot was taking a holiday in France, she saw the spirit body of her dog before she heard of the animal's "death" in England. Mrs. Bagot was staying at the Hotel des Anglais at Mentone when the psychic incident occurred.

Before leaving England, she had left Judy, her little black and tan terrier, at home in the care of the gardener.

Sitting in the dining-room of her hotel, Mrs. Bagot suddenly saw her dog run across the floor. Unthinkingly, she exclaimed, "Why, there's Judy!"

There was no dog in the hotel. When Mrs. Bagot went upstairs to see her daughter, who was ill, she told her of this experience.

A few days later she received a letter telling her that Judy had been suddenly taken ill and had since "died." The dog had been quite well even on the morning of her "death." She had gone out with the gardener in the usual way, but was taken ill after they returned to the house at breakfast-time. Within half an hour, Judy had passed on.

Mrs. Bagot later reported her experience to the Society for Psychical Research. She concluded her statement with these words, "At this distance of time I cannot distinctly remember whether the dates agreed, but my impression is that she had died the day I saw her."

Mrs. Wodehouse, the daughter of Mrs. Bagot, referred to her mother's psychic vision in her diary where she stated, "Mamma saw Judy's ghost at table d'hôte." This part of her diary was written when she was with her mother at Mentone.

A few days later, her mother visited her after she had left Mentone and was staying at Monte Carlo. In her diary appears the following, "Mamma and A. came over for the day. Judy dead, poor old dear."

Mrs. Wodehouse later amplified her entry in the diary by saying, "I distinctly remember my father and mother and sister and my cousin coming into my bedroom all laughing and telling me how my mother had seen Judy running across the room. My mother was so positive about it, that one of the others (I *think* my father) had asked the waiter if there were any dogs in the hotel, and he had answered in the negative. I can find no further mention of the time or day of the dog's death in my diary.

"I may also be mistaken in the day on which my mother saw Judy, for although I usually write my diary every evening, I sometimes leave it for two or three days and then write it as best I can remember. But I *distinctly* remember lying in my bed at Mentone when they told me the story, and equally clearly I remember receiving the news of Judy's death at Monte Carlo."

In referring to Mrs. Wodehouse's statement, F. W. H. Myers, the famous psychic investigator, wrote, "It will be observed that there is no proof that the dog was seen on the day of its death, but it is clear that Mrs. Bagot had not heard of its death till afterwards."

This carefully investigated case contains incontestable proof that the spirit body of the dog was seen by Mrs. Bagot before she was informed of the animal's "death."

Mrs. A. M. Liddell's little Pekingese, Bubbles, had an unusually deep bark for such a small dog.

Just after his earthly body was buried, his owner heard the sound of his characteristic bark just outside the room. So distinct was the sound that she called to her husband who was in another part of the house, "Is Bubbles really 'dead'?" He replied, "Of course he is. I saw him in rigor mortis myself!" Nevertheless he, too, admitted that he heard the dog's bark at the same time as his wife. The sound also reached the ears of one of the maids in the kitchen, although a second maid who was with her heard nothing!

Almost two years after the incident, a friend came to stay at the house. It was her first visit, and she knew nothing about Bubbles. When Mrs. Liddell went into her visitor's room the following morning, her guest's first words were, "This house is haunted!"

She went on to say that she had been lying wide awake when she suddenly heard a deep bark at the side of the bed. She imitated the unusual bark of Bubbles perfectly. "I have never been so frightened in my life," she said. "I switched on the light, jumped out of bed and searched the room for the dog."

Mrs. Liddell explained that it must have been Bubbles who had disturbed her. In his earthly life, the Peke was in the habit of visiting this particular guest room whenever there was an occupant. Bubbles would always greet the visitor with his deep bark of welcome.

However, the "dead" dog paid no further calls on the guest whom he had unwittingly frightened by the repetition of his habitual greeting.

On several occasions after his cattle dog was killed in Canada, Mr. C. Hammersley found, when he went for his cattle, that the animals would begin to move and bunch together, as though the dog was there helping him as usual. This continued until he got another dog. "But at times," says Mr. Hammersley, "it happens even now.

He also describes how his brother was protected from thieves by a "dead" dog. One dark night, when his brother was coming home from town along a lonely road, he heard a noise. Looking backwards, he saw two men following him, apparently intent on robbery.

At the same moment, however, a large black dog suddenly came to the side of the pursued man. An oath came from one of the men, and they both slunk away. When his brother reached the gate which led to his home, he turned and patted the dog who had so adequately protected him. But while he was caressing the animal it vanished into thin air!

In my own flat, the shadowy form of our first cat, Snoopy, is sometimes seen for a fleeting moment.

Once, during Snoopy's earthly life, he disappeared from home for over a week. I was so distressed that, at our weekly home circle, I asked the guides whether, if the cat was not already "dead," they would try to bring him back. They said they would do their utmost to find out what had happened to him.

They succeeded! The day after the sitting we found a thin, unkempt Snoopy sitting outside the door of the flat. He was in a dazed, almost trance-like condition. We could not induce him to eat or drink until several hours later, when he had recovered from his strange stupor.

I do not know by what means Snoopy was returned to us, but I am convinced that it was due to spirit agency.

The spirit world does not despise even the services of little four-legged creatures to help prove to this world that there is no death. The medium, Mr Harold Sharp, used to sit regularly with four other Spiritualists in a home circle where a table was used for the purpose of communicating with the spirit world. As I have previously described, spirit messages are received at this kind of séance by means of raps or tilting of the table, each corresponding to a letter in the alphabet.

One evening, just when the sitting was drawing to a close, the following message was received, "Harold—rescue the perishing. Even the little one has an important part to play in destiny."

At that time, Mr. Sharp was actively engaged in helping Mrs. A. Appleby, a Spiritualist who nightly fed hundreds of the destitute on the Embankment and in Trafalgar Square. He concluded that the message referred in some way to this activity.

The sitting came to an end. After the inevitable "cup of tea" which follows the close of most home circles almost as regularly as night follows day, the members of the group prepared to leave.

Opening the front door, they found that snow had fallen since their arrival. Sitting in the snow outside the house was a little tabby cat. It appeared to be lost.

"Wherever do you belong?" asked Mr. Sharp as he picked it up. Whereupon the cat began to purr contentedly, but unfortunately was unable to answer this rather important question.

Mr. Sharp looked searchingly at the cat in his arms and said to his friends, "I know I've seen this tabby sitting on a gateway of a house in Hendon Way. I'll take it along and see if I can find its home." Hendon Way was two miles away, and his friends tried to dissuade him from going there on the slender chance that the cat really was the one he had seen. "You'll only get the cat more thoroughly lost than ever," they said. "How do you know it's the same one you saw on the gatepost? Why, all tabby cats look alike!"

What a statement to make to a cat-lover! It simply made Mr. Sharp more determined than before to confirm his belief that he *had* seen this particular little tabby cat elsewhere. So he tucked it comfortably under his arm and set off for Hendon Way. When he arrived at the house, it was in complete darkness. He rang the bell several times before the door was finally opened by a man.

"Is this your cat?" asked the medium.

It was!

The owner was delighted and in a subsequent conversation told Mr. Sharp that the tabby's name was "Little One"—because it was so tiny. When he heard this, the medium informed him about the spirit message he had received earlier that night which had referred to the "Little One."

The man became interested. He said he knew very little about Spiritualism but sorely needed consolation. One after another, his beloved family had passed on—his mother, his wife, and his child.

Mr. Sharp remained with him for more than an hour that night, telling him some of the facts of Survival.

At a later date the man investigated these facts for himself. He attended a séance held by Mrs. Helen Duncan where his little boy materialised in front of him. How happy it made this man, when the "dead" child explained, "I brought 'Little One' out, Dad, because we wanted you to know…"

Many famous men have given their testimony to animal survival. Sir Arthur Conan Doyle has told how a medium, coming into his study, clairvoyantly saw, and successfully described, the author's "dead" dog to him.

Sir Oliver Lodge, drawing on his almost sixty years of psychic investigation, once wrote, "I have often been asked about the survival of animals. Well, affection is the most vital thing in life and, like other vital realities, it continues. The universe is governed by love more than by anything else, and no reality of that kind fades out of existence.

"We have high authority for figurative statements emphasising this, such as that the hairs of our heads are numbered, and that not a sparrow falls to the ground without the knowledge of the Heavenly Father.

"Life itself does not go out of existence, but only leaves its association with matter. Ordinary plants and animals have acquired no individuality, and therefore for them there is no individual survival. The higher animals, however, have developed some human qualities. They have attained a stage at which there is individual memory, which is the beginning of personality. Some of them have attained a stage at which love for their human friends is dominant."

The "Grand Old Man" of Science declared that his "dead" son Raymond "tells me that his favourite dog came to welcome him, and that he and others are not cut off from their animal friends. Love is not an evanescent but an enduring thing, and a time of reunion may be confidently looked for.

"The particular shape of the body matters little. It is the soul and the faculties that survive, when they really and truly exist. Some four-footed creatures seem to me to have attained that stage. The evidence or testimony is that survival in their case is a reality."

CHAPTER XVII

LIFE IN THE NEXT WORLD

THERE is enough evidence to prove conclusively that the higher animals survive "death" as individual personalities because of their association with man.

How long they continue to survive in animal form may be conditioned by other factors. It may be determined by the degree of consciousness they have attained. It may be governed by the strength of the ties that bind them to human beings.

As time, or its equivalent in the spirit world, goes by, it is quite likely that the links that have bound an animal to a human being may weaken for different reasons.

The survival of animals *as* animals may not have the same permanent quality as man's, nor may our lesser brethren have the unlimited scope of eternal progress toward perfection that is open to humans.

This does not mean that progress is not available even to God's lowliest creatures. But their evolution may lie in different directions, not necessarily in association with man.

Many people believe that animals reincarnate, in time, as human beings. Sometimes one wonders whether this may be considered progression or retrogression! These questions are matters for speculation because they cannot be proved in the same way as personal survival.

Nevertheless, certain highly evolved spirits, for whose wisdom we have the greatest respect, have given us their opinions on some of these matters. I put a number of germane questions to a well known guide. In a later chapter they are dealt with more fully.

But, leaving the realm of speculation, it may be accepted as a fact that, while the ties of love link an animal to a human, the contact is maintained in the next world so long as the association is desired.

If a human and his animal friend have both passed on, they may not possibly spend the whole of their time together. Do not the same conditions exist even on this earth? The daily routine of life and work usually necessitate a certain amount of separation from our human loved ones as well as our pets.

It is usually stressed by spirit communicators that there are no barriers to divide humans and animals from being together in the next world, when this association is mutually desired.

You will remember that when Mr. Holland Hennequin told his "dead" son Eddie at a sitting that their dog Dinkie would soon pass over, the boy replied that the dog would join him in the spirit world. "When he comes," said Eddie, "he will share my home here until you and Mum come."

If the tie of love still binds, there is no doubt that an animal who has passed on will be greeted and cared for by those human friends who have preceded him to the spirit world.

A domestic pet who "dies" before his owner is often taken under the special care of a human spirit linked in sympathy with the owner. Such a human spirit would naturally help the one on earth by doing all that was possible for the animal who has passed on.

Dr. Margaret Vivian told in "Psychic News" how, when she asked her spirit friend "F.R." about her dog who had recently "died," he said, "I have him. He is with you often... He will survive until you also come here and after. Quite special care is taken of your dog and of others by those who, like myself, have always loved them."

Apart from such cases where a "dead" pet is taken under the personal care of a spirit friend or relative of his owner, there are many who may not be able to make such a contact.

Such animals are not neglected, you may be sure. There are humans in the spirit world whose labour of love is to look after the lesser brethren who pass on, and help them accustom themselves to their new conditions. A dog would feel very strange in a new world where there were no human beings with whom to associate.

Not only those who have had domestic association with man, but all species of animals go, when they "die," to the part of the spirit world known as the animal plane, or sphere. They gravitate quite naturally to the particular spirit environment most suited to their needs, state of consciousness, and conditions of passing.

It is perhaps necessary to explain, to those who may wonder about the various planes in the next world, that these spheres are not territories in the geographical sense of the word. They are differing conditions or degrees of environment, attracting the appropriate spirit to its own sphere of existence.

These spheres, inhabited by those most suited to them, may, however, be visited by spirits who normally dwell on a different plane. Thus, spirit people whose evolution has earned them a higher sphere, comparatively speaking, often travel to a lower plane to help the ones who dwell there.

Some spirit people visit, and even live on the animal plane in order to work there.

They find happiness and contentment in being allowed to minister to the varying needs of the "dead" animals who require human companionship or help. Some domestic pets who have recently passed to the spirit world before their owners may need sympathy and comfort from a human.

It may be the work of other helpers on the animal plane to assist a pet to make contact with his owner still on earth, and help prove to the sorrowing human left behind that the beloved animal is very much alive.

Then again, perhaps as compensation for the amount of wild animal life he thoughtlessly destroyed while on earth, it might be a human's lot to render aid to the newly awakened spirits of slaughtered beasts. He may assist the bewildered cattle, recently slain for food, to become fully alive to their new form of existence. He may lead them to "pastures new" where contentment awaits them, and where they will never again know the sudden agony of being done to death by the hand of a human being.

In the perfect operation of divine law, both man and beast

must receive compensation in the next sphere for what they have suffered on earth as innocent victims of injustice.

You may perhaps ask what happens to those "dead" animals who have had no opportunity of acquiring even a small degree of individual consciousness through association with human beings.

What happens, for instance, to the timid untamed creatures, to the wild birds of the air, to the myriads of insects? What happens to ferocious beasts and to verminous pests? What becomes of cattle and other creatures who have had no association with man except for purposes of being reared and later slaughtered for food or sport?

There is no evidence that they survive as individual spirits in the same way as those higher animals who have attained individual consciousness.

Yet even the very lowest forms of life have some form of survival because we know that the living spark cannot be extinguished by the death of the physical form.

Because such creatures are not sufficiently evolved to prove their continued existence to us, we have to rely on what we are told by those on the Other Side whose opinions we have learned to respect.

And although opinions of spirit communicators may differ on certain points about the kind of survival of lowly, forms of life, in the main there is agreement on the points that matter.

It is generally understood that all creatures passover to their own particular sphere on the animal plane. Nevertheless, we are told that ferocious beasts, for example, do not continue to prey upon other animals, because they no longer feel the necessity for fulfilling carnivorous appetites. For similar reasons, the unpleasant characteristics of verminous pests cease to manifest.

We are told that the lower forms of life become part of a "group soul" when their physical life is over. This group soul has its own useful functions to perform, for there is no wastage in the operation of God's law.

Questions on this subject were put to the guide of our own home circle, and appear with his answers in another chapter.

Descriptions of the animal spheres have been received through various forms of spirit communication. In automatic writing, through the hand of Mr. E. E. Green, a spirit known as Lampbearer has given an account of a visit he made to the animal plane. His description is included in the medium's book, "Lampbearer."

This spirit says that the animal plane is a small world, complete in itself. He tells how, when he visited this sphere, he beheld all kinds of dumb creatures, domestic and otherwise. He also saw certain species that he had never before encountered.

While he was watching and admiring the animals there, he saw several children playing with their pets. Some of the boys jumped on the backs of their horses and led them to Lampbearer to be fondled. The horses rubbed their heads against their playfellows, and seemed to convey the fact that they knew all that was going on around them.

He describes how the dogs bounded forward to greet him and they, too, expected their share of affection. He says, "They were of all kinds and sizes, some small, others somewhat bigger, while a considerable number were of the large kind who had been both workers and useful companions to their owners, who often visited them."

It was explained to Lampbearer by the spirit guide who was conducting him through this sphere that the animals did not spend the whole of their time with their human owners. He said that might interfere with other services that had to be rendered.

Lampbearer encountered cats of varying kinds, as well as many other domestic pets. The guide told him that all the animals came under the guardianship of spirits specially suited to this task.

After crossing a river which ran through this animal kingdom, Lampbearer was conducted by the guide to a region inhabited by birds. He heard rare notes and harmonies in this atmosphere of song. Most of the birds wore glorious plumage, and sang melodiously in praise of their Divine Creator.

The guide explained to Lampbearer that the trees here formed a natural haven of sanctuary for the birds. There were flowers, also, to provide the nectar of life for them.

Before his visit to this sphere, Lampbearer had no idea that animals had souls. When he expressed astonishment on learning this fact, the guide answered, "Neither have they such souls as we, but it is agreed that they have a second self, more or less a replica of their animal self, as the soul is a replica of the human when encased in the physical. The inner self is an advancing reality like unto yours or mine, but of a lower grade, if I may so put it. Their anima, or life essence, is nevertheless a spark from the same Divine Anvil as that of humanity, but because it has been made to flow through a different kind of channel its development is on a different plane. Thus they are subject to man's rule, even in this realm."

CHAPTER XVIII

SPIRIT GUIDE ANSWERS QUESTIONS

S ILVER BIRCH is the name of the Indian spirit guide of the circle to which I belong.

"Psychic News" regularly publishes accounts of the teachings of this guide as received through the lips of his entranced medium. Because his simple truths are read by people all over the globe, Silver Birch is beloved by many thousands.

This Indian guide has an eloquent tongue, but his teachings are so simple that a child can understand the truths he propounds.

Ministers of different religious denominations, well-known public figures, journalists, men of letters, people from all parts of the world have, at one time or another, visited this circle.

Yet I have never known Silver Birch to be confounded by a question, or to be at a loss to reply, in simple but eloquent language, to any problem presented to him.

You may wonder how a simple Red Indian, even though he be a "dead" one, may have acquired so much profound knowledge of the "Law" which he teaches.

Actually, many spirit guides merely use the "personality" of a "dead" Indian because the Indians were, in their past prime, masters of psychic force.

This "astral cloak," therefore, often covers the identity of a highly evolved spiritual being, whose real name might perhaps prove a little too much for those on this earth who listen to his teachings.

"One day I will tell you who I am," Silver Birch once said to us. "I had to come in the form of a humble Indian to win your love and devotion, not by the use of any high-sounding name, but to prove myself by the truth of what I taught. That is the Law."

Because I knew Silver Birch's views on animal survival would be illuminating and helpful, he was asked a number of questions in order that his answers might be included in this book.

Here are the questions, and his replies to them:

Do some animals spend their whole time with their human friends on the Other Side or is their real home on the animal sphere?

It depends, because love is the index. You know that love determines the survival of animals. It is the love that exists between the animal and the person that enables the animal to obtain the temporary consciousness that exists beyond the grave of matter.

If an animal and—I do not like the word "owner," because no one owns another soul—the one whom it has served are in the world of spirit together, then the home of the animal is the home of the individual who has always loved it. It stays where love is, for love is the link that binds it to the one who loves it. It has no necessity to go to the animal plane, because it has its home.

Those who dwell in the animal sphere are the ones who come to the world of spirit before the masters, or owners, as you call them, arrive in our world, because it is necessary that someone shall take care of them. Otherwise they would be distracted, being cut off from the love which not only warmed their hearts but breathed a temporary immortality into them.

Where the animal comes to our world preceding the one who loved it, who gave it shelter and taught it all the habits of memory, of reason, of judgment and affection, it goes to the animal world to await the time when it can greet the one it has missed. There it is put in the charge of those specially trained to look after animals, just as you have trainers in your world to care for animals when their masters and mistresses are away.

Will you describe what it is an animal obtains from human contact that makes it survive?

In the long line of evolution, at some stage the Great Spirit, or the Law, breathed into animal and it became a living soul, conscious, aware of its own existence. Then came the dawn of reason; intelligence bloomed; there was judgment, the ability to reflect, to decide, to weigh and to consider. But, potentially, all that existed—no matter how far back in the line of evolution you go. It required the breath of the Great Spirit to awaken it.

Just as the Great Spirit enabled a divine spark to become a flame, so you, by love, transfer that process to the animal who lives within the shelter of your affection. You are part of the Great Spirit, having the power within you to transfer the attribute of spirit to the next in the line of evolution, so that by your association, by radiating love, you awaken that consciousness which, in time, through the process of evolution, would reach its own apex.

Love is the keynote in all life. Death cannot still the voice of love in humans or in animals. Love is the driving force throughout the whole universe; love directs all life; love controls and governs all life; and love seeks to work through man towards all other creatures, whether they be his equals or his inferiors.

The love that emanates from man to the lesser beings he embraces in his heart—the dog, the cat and the pets—cannot be ended by "death." It is love that determines that life must go on because love goes on.

How long does the survival of an animal last? Is it as long as that of a human being?

No, there is this difference. At some stage the animal and the human evolution inevitably part company. It may take, as you measure time, hundreds or thousands of years, but their rates of spiritual evolution are unequal. The animal has to be left behind because it cannot keep pace with the growing soul that restlessly struggles towards the greater light.

Once you have passed from the veil of matter and accustomed yourself to conditions of the spiritual life, once you have realised that the ties which bind you to earth are severed, the desire to progress, the desire to unfold the surging divinity within becomes quickened. You seek to unfold all the qualities which, by their practice, will enable you to be of greater service wherever you are. The higher you climb in that realm of spiritual unfoldment, the more difficult is it for the animal to keep pace with you. And so the love which kindled for a while a flame that burned beyond "death" gradually becomes attenuated. The flame flickers and it merges in the end with the group soul of that species.

Does that mean that the animal loses its personality and individuality?

Yes. That is the clear distinction between the two evolutions, because the animal, as a group, has not yet reached the stage of evolution when the whole group is individualised. Otherwise it would cease to be animal; it would then have reached the stage of the human being. But because you enable it to jump the scale of evolution, because you enable it to advance by love, it means that it must return to the group out of which it is formed.

It sounds rather unfair that, because the animal has earned individuality for itself, it must return and lose what it has gained.

No, because it has contributed to the group spirit and has enabled the process of evolution to be advanced by its fraction of evolution. It contributes to the common stock. It adds a quota to the pool that before did not exist. It makes the sacrifice of the one in order to help the whole. The more such sacrifices are made, the quicker the group soul advances towards the stage where it leaves the animal behind and earns the evolution which makes it now ready for individual souls in human form.

Is that when they definitely become incarnated?

There are two kinds of incarnation. There is the old soul re-embodied in the world of matter and there is what you call the "new soul," starting its first phase in the world of matter as an individual.

Do you mean as a human individual?

Yes. They are both spirit, they are both conscious spirit, they are both individual spirit. But one is an old soul, returning to complete or help complete a cycle; the other is a new soul on the first rung of the ladder. The new one comes from the group, the group that once was animal, the pool of spirit which has been through all the evolutionary stages of animal, of bird, of fish, of reptile, right back to the lowest slime on earth.

That is Theosophical teaching.

I do not care whose belief it is. You should not tell me about labels. I am not interested.

All these facetious critics who do not desire knowledge, who only seek to exhibit their vaunted intelligence, do not realise the simple truth. You do not bring a spider into your home and give it love, do you? You do not bring a beetle into your home and give it love and try to serve it. You do not give it companionship and the warmth of your heart, do you?

No, because you recognise the gulf that is fixed between you, because you know instinctively that it is far away from you in the scale of evolution. You bring those whom you call the domestic animals-the dog, the cat, sometimes the monkey—because you feel a kinship with them. They are just below you in the line of evolution. They are ready for your love or affection because they are awaiting the next stage in their evolution, which is incarnation as humans.

Where lower animals are brought into the home, does it mean they are ready for it?

There are off shoots, the advance guard of evolution, and there are throw-backs, the rearguard of evolution. Always there are examples of what goes before and what comes behind. There are always exceptions. You may find the unintelligent animal which is a retrograde; you may find the intelligent bird which is in advance of the dog. But do not seek to confuse the general principle with exceptional cases.

Do parts of the pool go through the same animal incarnation only once, or several times?

Once. The pool is added to by the increasing endeavours of those who contribute to it. There is no necessity for the pool to return; otherwise it cannot be progressing.

Would it be desirable to extend to all living creatures the love we give to dogs and cats?

Yes, but do not expect the same response from those who are lower in the scale of evolution. Love will kindle love, hatred will beget hatred. But remember that the lower in the scale you go the less response can you expect. If there is anger in your heart, it is only a criticism of your own self, your own lack of development, your own imperfection, for when you have got rid of anger, of malice, of hatred, of rage, of envy, then you are on the high road to spiritual attainment.

If part of a group incarnated as humans and was a dismal failure, would it return to the animal pool?

No, because once there is individual consciousness as *a* human being it can never be extinguished. It is your bond with the Great Spirit that can never be severed.

How does the law of compensation work in the case of slaughtered and ill-treated animals?

There is compensation, but it is a compensation that affects the group spirit and not the animal that has been slaughtered. The law of compensation and retribution applies in different forms to unevolved animals and humans. The animal, having to go into the group spirit, cannot be subjected in our world, to a law which can compensate it when it no longer exists as an individual. There is a compensation within the group, but I regret I have no means of describing it. There is nothing similar in your earthly life with which to compare it.

Some people say that verminous pests, such as lice and bugs, are the results of man's evil thoughts. Is that true, or are they the result of natural causes, such as dirt and disease?

But what causes dirt and disease? Are they not, at some stage or other, attributable to man's selfishness, which could be called his evil thoughts? The actual physical cause is to be found in bad sanitation, in foul breeding grounds, in needless dirt and disease, in wrongful conditions, lack of sunshine and clean air. The cause for these things is to be found in man's selfishness to man, man's inhumanity to man, which you might describe as his evil thoughts or, as I would say, his lack of development. But get rid of the selfishness, get rid of the idea of exploitation, get rid of the system which breeds avarice and greed, and you will get rid of what you call your pests or vermin.

That cannot be applicable in the case of, say, mosquitoes.

You must remember that the whole of the world of nature is still subject to the law of evolution, that nature's balance is constantly altering in accordance with the people who dwell in this world, and that the more humanity evolves the less of nature's darkness will be found in the world. There is a relationship between the growth of man's spirit and the natural phenomena of the countries in which man dwells.

You cannot dismiss man from his environment and you cannot dismiss man's growth from the phenomena of nature which surround his environment. The development is almost on parallel lines. Man, being part of creation, being part of the Great Spirit, being a co-sharer with the Great Spirit in the work of the universe, also contributes to the natural laws which control his own life, even his national life. There is a gap—I said *almost* on parallel lines—because the influence of older generations has to be outworked in time.

Do your comments also refer to ferocious and wild beasts?

Partly, but remember that evolution is not static. It is a continuous and eternal progress. There is always a growth from the rudimentary forms through the lower to the higher. The lower of yesterday becomes the higher of today, and the higher of today becomes the lower of tomorrow.

Is there, then, retrogression in evolution?

Yes, if you term it retrogression, because the evolution is accomplished in cycles, or, as your modern philosophers now think, in spirals. It does not matter how you express it as long as you realise it is not a straight line all the time. There is an advance, a falling back; a greater advance, a falling back, continuously.

As animals kill each other, why should not we kill them in such experiments as vivisection?

Because that is the expression of human evolution. As human evolution advances so ferocity and brutishness dies out and becomes extinct. When mankind has reached the stage when love and kindness and tolerance are accepted by all there will be no ferocity among the animals. Indeed, the lion will lie down with the lamb.

Isn't cruelty part of the law of development in animals?

Do you not see that once you were animal, and that is the expression of the evolution that was you? That is why there is less and less ferocity, less cruelty amongst the animals of nature. Where are the saurians of yesterday? Why are they extinct? Because there has been evolution of man.

A lot of the non ferocious animals have become extinct too.

I mean that the true level was ferocity. There were the off-shoots even in those times. They were the precursors of the evolutionary line. Evolution is not static at any stage. You have the precursors and the renegades, those who are advanced—and those who are behind. The "non-ferocious" ones were the precursors that had outgrown the "breathing fire" ones.

Do the verminous pests join the same group as the higher animals?

No.

There is not only one group soul, then?

No. There is a group for every species.

Are not these groups subdivided?

Yes. There is a group for every subdivision of the species. The new spirit—if there is the incarnation of one who has never re-embodied—comes from the highest of the animal group.

That again is in a kind of cycle?

Yes, it is all in cycles.

Which is the highest of the animal group?

The dog.

Does the pest group soul have a harmful effect?

No, because compared with the balance it is infinitesimal. You must remember you are now asking deeper questions that are not usually touched upon.

Is the group soul situated on the animal planes?

I have one great advantage over you. I do not have to learn lessons in geography. We have no situations. Space is, boundless and spiritual conditions do not occupy space. You are thinking in terms of physical location and spirit does not require a habitation, unless it is to assume form. But a group soul requires no form. When it does, then it has to have a mode of manifestation and a place where that mode is manifested.

Do the group souls supply any physical forces to this world? Are they of any use to this world?

Only in the process of evolution. You must remember that you are trying to differentiate between things physical and spiritual. Whatever is alive in your world is already part of the group soul, even though it is still in your world, so that it does not have to die to join the group soul.

Do pet animals visit the spirit world in sleep? No. Are they not familiar with it when they pass?

No. When in your sleep state you come to our world you do so because you have your guides to take you by the hand. But none can do that for the animal except the one it knows, and that one is still in the world of matter.

Suppose that one had passed on?

That is a little different, but I speak generally.

Why are animals, particularly cats and dogs, often more psychic than human beings?

Because although they have not as yet, as far as evolution goes, reached the stage where they become humans, they have not had to face the "civilised" life that human beings do. If the human had not had the "benefits" of what you call "civilisation," then before now he would have reached the stage where the exercise of psychic qualities was part of his normal life. He has sacrificed that for his "civilisation."

The animal, not faced with the economic problems, with the sociological problems that effect human beings, has continued in the evolutionary line to the stage that humans should have reached, but have not, and therefore is in possession of those psychic qualities which humans have, but often repress, because of the material life they have to lead.

Then again, those whom you call mediums are the precursors of the evolutionary line. They are exhibiting today what will be natural tomorrow.

Animals have what is called a sixth sense-they have premonitions and the ability to find their way over unknown territory. Is that a psychic quality?

Yes, that is what mediums can do also. But sometimes it is a quality of the species because, there again, you get a precursion of evolution manifest in one quality, like the pigeon, which has developed the one quality of finding its way home. It is called instinct, but it is really a form of lucidity. They are qualities *which* are precursors to the line of evolution.

Sometimes when a medium describes a "dead" animal, it is accompanied by another one. Does one animal help the other to return?

No, unless there was an association between the two animals already in your earthly world.

Is it always a human spirit who helps them?

Yes, because the higher helps the lower always. It is the Law.

What sort of animals are on the animal plane?

All those animals which were your pets, which you thought to be almost your equals, which you endowed with affection, with love, and stimulated their reason and their ability to think. Rather than that they should be lonely, disconsolate, lost without the one to whom they were attached, they come to this plane where they mingle with other animals and receive the special care of those who, having devoted their lives to the study of animals, are able to minister to them and to give them the kindness which is their natural expression.

In this world they find all the things that will delight animals, all the pursuits of enjoyment that prevent them from fretting. And occasionally they are brought within the radius of the home, so that they can still feel the affection of the ones from whom they are parted for a while. That is why so many sometimes see or hear the dog or the cat, even though they do not possess a knowledge of Spiritualism. They only know that there is a sense, or feeling, that the dog is there. And other animals always see them because of their higher psychic qualities.

Do the spirit people who work on the animal plane bring them back?

It is the ones who minister to them on the animal plane who bring them back because they would not come back with anybody else. And do you know who are the ones who minister to them? Those who were passionately devoted to animals and never had the opportunity of befriending them, just as in our world the children who pass before their parents are cared for by those who had strong maternal instincts which were never satisfied.

The dogs and the cats and all the pets are cared for by those who were devoted to them and did not have the means of lavishing their devotion upon them. Of course, they are aided by those who have specialised knowledge of animals, which is always used in our world. Knowledge is never wasted.

If an animal is ill when it passes over, does it get nursed, as human beings do ?

Yes, because there are many in our world who are glad to have the opportunity.

Are there different sections, or do the animals mingle?

No, the boundaries are fixed.

Though it is one animal plane, has it different boundaries?

Yes. It is very natural. It is not like a huge pen.

Are cats separated from the dogs?

Yes, they are.

Except the friendly ones, and I suppose they are near the boundaries?

Yes, it is all very natural.

Which is next in the line of animal evolution after the dog—the cat or the monkey?

The cat.

Why not the monkey, considering he is so much like us?

Evolution, as I have tried to explain, is not in a straight line. There are always precursors and retrogrades. Whilst man has developed in his line of evolution from the monkey, that pace has not been maintained and the dog has passed the monkey stage, largely because man has conferred friendship on the dog.

I thought man gave his affection to the dog because it was next in the line.

But at the same time man has his choice, as he is part of Creation. There is another aspect which is very complicated and hard to explain.

At one epoch in the long line of evolution, the ascending monkeys slipped back and became, not ferocious, but quarrelsome and lazy, and neglected to continue their progress. The result was, that the whole "group spirit" was retarded. At the same time, or more or less at the same time, the dog section advanced because there was a greater co-operation and a spirit of unselfishness. But I am afraid that is too complicated.

Did the monkeys break the Law?

They did not break the Law, but they failed to live up to what they could have done.

Is it possible that in the future the dog will slip backwards?

No, I do not think so, because now, after all these millions of years, the species have become defined. The pattern has become almost standardised and the chances of physical evolution are diminishing. You must remember that there is a limit to physical evolution, in the sense that there can be changes in form, but not in the essential pattern. There can be variations but not complete changes.

For example, take your physical body. You will not outgrow, for generations, this form, this shape-the two arms, two eyes, one nose, two legs. That pattern has now become fairly standardised. There will be variations according to race and country, but not changes in the pattern. This is more so in regard to the animals, so that there will be an emergence of the group spirit in the animal world but not so much in the physical world.

Would the slipping backwards of the monkey be the result of free will?

No, because it is a condition that affects the whole group.

How could the group will decide if it had no individual' consciousness?

There is a difference between the behaviour of animals according to their instincts and also lack of instincts. Even in animals, where there is no individual reasoning ability, there is a power either for labour or for idleness. It can respond, or fail to respond. Itt can sharpen or awaken the instincts of the group. And, though it has no individual judgment, there can be, in the line of evolution, epoch where the whole species is failing to respond to what it is capable of doing.

Does that apply to plants too?

Yes.

Could not that be caused by external conditions?

Yes, but what you call external conditions are internal too. Then, added to the complications is the fact that there is also the work of those who regulate and control these phases of life from our world. They too are subject to law, to initiative and to progress.

If, for instance, nuts were plentiful, would that make the monkeys lazy?

Yes, but if nuts were plentiful it would be because of a law which would operate in the universe and, whilst it might be external to the world of matter, it would be internal to the world of spirit. That was the point I was trying to establish.

You must not visualise the Law as being a rigid, mechanical, automatic, lifeless process. There is always an interplay of forces, themselves subject to law, but it is a law that operates with intelligence, controlled from the centre, directed from the source by infinite perfect intelligence.

There is a pattern, but there can be variations. You cannot go outside the pattern. If you make a tangle, the pattern is still there and ultimately you must conform to the pattern. You can make the pattern richer or poorer; you can introduce harmonious or inharmonious colours. The pattern must come right in the end.

• • • • •

At the end of these questions the guide made this comment:

"Just as animals strive to serve us with devotion, let us always try to serve others with equal devotion, with equal faithfulness, for it is all part of the divine love restlessly stirring which seeks to find expression everywhere. In a world that is so full of hatred and anger and jealousy, rage and fierce passion, it is increasingly necessary for divine love to be made manifest."

On another occasion, Silver Birch answered a series of questions on the moral aspects of experiments on living animals. Here are the questions and the guide's replies:

How do you view the ever-increasing practice of experiments, on living animals, often causing terrible pain to helpless creatures? Many people on this side are striving to get this unholy thing stopped. Are they helped in any way from the spirit world?

All those who desire to serve at once bring to their aid those in: my world who will inspire and sustain and bring them the power of the spirit to aid the work they seek to do. It is, wrong, to administer pain to any of the creatures of the Great Spirit, but you must remember that there are many who do it in ignorance, not realising the pain that they inflict, only possessed with motives to help their fellow men. But they are still breaking the Law.

But if, as we are often told, only the motive counts, will those people who inflict pain in what they conceive to be service to their fellow men have to pay the penalty for breaking the Law?

The motives may be good, but the principle is unaltered.. If one deliberately inflicts pain, knowing it will hurt, that means that the one who does it is conscious of his responsibility. His motives, of course, are good, but he has inflicted pain. All these facts are taken into account, but I cannot agree with the practice of inflicting pain.

Are animals sent to earth to help mankind?

Yes. And mankind is sent to help them.

But the sole purpose of the animal creation is not to be of use to man.

No, that is only part of the work.

Do you believe that vivisection can be right when it is undertaken with a good motive?

No. How can that which is cruel be right? How can that which causes pain, which inflicts torture, be right? It is contrary to all we teach. It is wrong to experiment on those who are not capable of resisting.

Do you agree that no cure for cancer will ever be_ found by that method?

Your world cannot produce remedies for the diseases which it has created by living contrary to the laws of the Great Spirit. There will be found remedies for all your diseases, but they will not be found by experiments on animals.

Why does not the spirit world interfere when it sees so many appalling atrocities committed on animals?

Because the universe is ruled by natural laws.

• • • • •

Once, Silver Birch was asked by a sitter, who had taken part in a fox shoot, whether he had done wrong.

"All life belongs to the Great White Spirit," replied the guide, "and no one must take it, in whatever form it is."

"But the fox had eaten twenty chickens."

"Suppose I gave the fox a gun and told him to shoot you because you had eaten twenty chickens. The Great White Spirit has provided for all His children everywhere. It is man who makes them starve, not the fox.

"When the children of earth have begun to evolve into higher beings, all their gross desires will fall away. When you can create the fox, or the chicken, then you can take its life away. If it is true that you can kill the chicken and the fox, then it is right for a man to kill his brother.

"Life does not belong to man. It belongs to the Great White Spirit. Whenever anyone takes it away, he must answer for it some day.

"What of the menace of rabbits in Australia?"

"You take something away from where it should be, and then you complain of the result. It was the same with the white man who came to my country. He also brought war, `firewater,' and many things that helped to bring sadness to the Indian. We did not know how to shoot with firearms until the white man came and he said it was right to kill.

"One day you will understand the law of the Father, which is that all things in the universe—animal, bird, fish or flower—are all parts of the Great White Spirit's plan. They are all there as parts of the creation of the Great White Spirit."

On another occasion, a member of the circle asked the following question, *"Why is it that in all the teachings of Jesus that have been recorded there is very little about animals?"*

"Because at the time in which he lived the human race had not yet evolved to that stage where there was concern over animal welfare."

"But animals are mentioned by other masters."

"Some of them came much later, though not all. But you must

try to realise that the Nazarene came to your world, not to be the one pattern for all humanity, but as an example to the western world. He came with a special mission to perform and, though he himself had compassion for every form of life, he knew his mission and strove to make it as simple as possible.

"His mission was to cut through the antiquated growth of creed that had for too long obstructed the world and to leave on record those simple practical teachings to serve as a searchlight to the western world."

"Do you think any teaching can be complete without regard for the lower creation?"

"No, 1 do not, but it is all in the Nazarene's teachings' if, you apply it. He taught the golden rule of love, and anyone who has love in his heart cannot be cruel to any form of life.

CHAPTER XIX

MAN—THE INCONSISTENT

WHAT an inconsistent creature is man—God's greatest success, God's biggest failure! Man can rise to noble and lofty heights; he can descend to the lowest pit of degradation.

Man—the inconsistent! Woe betide the stranger who would harm one hair of the head of his dog, the beloved four-footed member of the household.

Yet the same man will turn a deaf ear to the cries of the same species of animal, tortured and maimed by cruel experiments on the vivisector's table. The thought of his *own* dog being so treated would be,enough to render him wild with indignation, grief and terror. Yet, the tortured beast is somebody's dog—or has been—or might have been!

If you were to point out this inconsistency to an ordinary, kindly man, he would probably agree with you. Nevertheless, he would say, "I know it is terrible and I prefer not to think about it. After all, vivisection is carried out for the sake of humanity. Think of the wonderful discoveries that would not otherwise have been made. Think of the alleviation of suffering that has been effected through experiments on animals; cures for diabetes, rabies, and all sorts of diseases have been obtained."

This kindly but thoughtless man has never taken the trouble to find out for himself exactly how slight a foundation of fact there is for such blind belief.

Such organisations as the Animal Defence Society have a vast amount of literature and data proving the fallacy of the claims made on behalf of vivisection. I must confess I was astounded when I learned how little foundation there was for these claims.

No lasting benefit to humanity can result from cruel exploitation of the weak. "That which is morally wrong can never be scientifically right," has been said with complete justification.

The cures for many of our ills lie in our midst, provided by nature's bounty. And numerous diseases would be prevented by the abolition of dirt and poverty. With a wider understanding, of sanitation and its application to our needs, many of the dread scourges would pass away.

It is certain that the infliction of suffering on helpless animals who possess feeling and faculties similar to our own will never conquer disease. Many of our ills have been brought about by our own betrayal of natural laws of health and life.

A clearer and wider understanding often comes to the spirit when it is released by death from the physical body. Sometimes such a spirit has been torn with remorse for the suffering he has thoughtlessly inflicted on animals.

Nina, Duchess of Hamilton and Brandon, is Chairman of the Council of the Animal Defence Society. She told in "Psychic News" how she once attended a seance where the tortured spirit of a repentant vivisector spoke to the sitters. He implored us, said the Duchess, "to continue to fight with all our strength the evil of vivisection for, he said, it is one of the strongest forces of evil that retard man's own evolution."

Personal responsibility comes with the knowledge that our spirits survive the death of the physical body. We know that we cannot escape the results of our earthly actions, and that our manner of life builds the character we take with us to the Other Side.

The Duchess of Hamilton is one of those who have put this knowledge into practical application. With Miss L. Lind-af-Hageby, Founder and President of the Animal Defence Society, and a number of other humanitarian women, she has worked with indefatigable zest towards the alleviation of every form of animal suffering.

These great workers for animal reform have visited slaughter houses in many countries. They have had to witness all kinds of horrible sights in order that they should be in a position to press for more humane methods of killing animals. Thanks to them, much success has been achieved in this direction.

They work untiringly on behalf of oppressed animals and, in addition, practically all humanitarian objects receive their unstinted support.

Sometimes I think of the welcome that will greet these women when they pass over and receive the reward of their untiring labours.

In my imagination, I see the hosts of animals who will press forward to greet the ones whose lives have been devoted to the alleviation of their suffering. I know that when they behold the gentle, trusting eyes of these dumb creatures it will be all the thanks, all the reward that such great souls will ever desire!

Man—the inconsistent! He will scold his child for teasing the dog or the cat. It is wrong to hurt animals, he will explain, because they feel pain and discomfort in the same way as humans. The little one will no doubt promise that in future he will protect helpless creatures, and treat them with kindness and consideration.

But one fine day the same child may be considered competent enough to mount a hunter. He will join a group of people similarly mounted. The men may be attired in picturesque scarlet coats and quaint little caps. There will be an air of excitement and thrill about this gathering.

A lot of dogs—I beg your pardon, I mean a pack of hounds—will add their quota of noise by their excited barking—I mean baying. Then, accompanied by a certain amount of ritualistic paraphernalia, the whole company will finally setoff on their objective. The concentrated effort of all these people is to chase to its destruction one small fox, and to get as much enjoyment out of the effort as they can.

Everything possible has been done to help these humans achieve their purpose, a good day's hunting with a "kill" at the end of it. For this reason, as many earth holes by which a fox might regain his underground home have been previously stopped up. If the quarry succeeds in eluding his pursuers, he may find the entrance to his sanctuary barred.

Even if the fox *does* succeed in finding some underground cover, the huntsmen will sometimes send terriers down to force him out into the open again. These terriers accompany the hunt expressly for this eventuality. The huntsmen do not intend to be deprived of the final satisfaction of the "kill," if they can help it. Failing this means of evicting the fox from his temporary refuge, he is often dug out by means of pick and spade.

Then, surrounded by those who have tracked him down, the broken creature, heart and lungs pitiably over-strained by the ordeal he has undergone, will be at the mercy of his pursuers.

Whether he reaches some temporary sanctuary and is dug out, or whether he is caught elsewhere, the end of the vanquished animal is the same. Amidst the baying of the excited hounds and the jubilation of the crowd, the life of the exhausted fox is extinguished.

Then follows a bloody ritual which is more in keeping with a savage ceremony to propitiate a god than a civilised custom.

The head and the tail of the fox are cut off by a huntsman and a person is chosen to receive the strange honour of being "blooded." To the accompaniment of the "twanging" of the huntsman's horn, the initiate is smeared on the face with the blood of the mutilated animal. Sometimes a child who has accompanied the hunt for the first time is the one chosen to be thus anointed and afterwards presented with the fox's tail—the brush—as a memento of the occasion.

It might be the same child who only recently was scolded for teasing another animal and told he must always protect helpless creatures.

Many people, brought up from infancy amongst such discrepancies in treatment of animals do not realise that they are being cruel and pitiless in indulging in killing for amusement. It never strikes them as inconsistent with their usual mode of living. They are usually kindly people, whose domestic pets are well treated, loved, and. sometimes pampered.

The fox has similar reactions to pain and distress as their own carefully nurtured animals at home.

But then, fox-hunting is "sport."

How elegant a woman looks in her furs! How becomingly the dead body of an animal frames a lovely face! Although a lover of dumb creatures, she has not thought of the torture the living body of the animal suffered in order that she might be so adorned.

Often, it is not until we are forced to consider our own thoughtless connivance in cruelty to animals that we realise our responsibilities.

Mrs. Gladys Osborne Leonard told in "Psychic News" how she once bought a fur coat which aroused her admiration. She confessed that she never seriously considered how the skins for the coat were obtained until she gave a sitting to her friend Sir Walter Gibbons.

It was a cold winter's day, and, before she went into trance, the medium put her fur coat over her knees. This act had disastrous results as far as the coat was concerned! After the sitting, Mrs. Leonard discovered that the garment had been torn to pieces by her guide Feda, a young girl. She asked Sir Walter what had occurred while she was in trance.

He said that no sooner had Feda controlled Mrs. Leonard's body than she broke off her cheerful welcome to him, and gave her attention to the fur coat on the medium's knees.

The next moment, with a cry of abhorrence and dismay, Feda exclaimed that she was "covered with dead animals." Tearing several pieces from the coat, she flung them violently as far away as possible.

In describing the incident Mrs. Leonard wrote, "How Feda found the strength to pull the coat apart so quickly and thoroughly I do not know. Urged by her, I afterwards took the trouble to investigate the methods used to obtain many furs, and was so impressed by the appalling cruelty involved that I have never since bought a fur of any description."

Man—the inconsistent! A father will take his children to feed the ducks and swans on the lake. Another time, he will go to Trafalgar Square, to St. Paul's, or some other open space and scatter corn to the fat, tame pigeons. He will throw breadcrumbs to the hungry sparrows.

In his own garden, he will have various arrangements and gadgets for feeding all kinds of birds. He will provide a bird bath for their further well-being.

Man will use every kind of device to protect the pheasants in his woods. They become so tame that they will eat out of the hand of the gamekeeper and answer to his whistle at feeding-time. All the animals that might be a menace to the pheasants are ruthlessly destroyed by steel trap and by gun.

Up to a certain day in the autumn, man has been such a friend to the pheasants that the birds have become tame and fat because they have not used their wings a great deal. After that date, man will take up his gun and kill as many of the birds as he can. It is for this purpose he has preserved their lives so carefully and at such an expense to his pocket!

Man—the inconsistent! Some of us will go into poetic rhapsodies at the picturesque sight of the lamb, gambolling by its mother's side on some green pasture-land. Then we will go home to eat, with thoughtless but hearty appetite, a "cut off the joint"—the lamb's joint!

How many thousands of turkeys and other birds are raised and reared for the express purpose of providing Christmas dinners? These creatures are slaughtered to help some of us celebrate the birth of Jesus of Nazareth, the man of compassion, born in a stable amongst the lowly animals.

Does it please him, I wonder, that so many creatures have to be slain in order to help Christians rejoice?

The earthbound spirit of a "dead" butcher, haunted by the memory of the hundreds of animals he had slaughtered in his lifetime, was once released from torment by Mr. Edward C. Randall, a famous New York attorney. The incident was described in "Psychic News."

Often an earthbound spirit cannot realise that he has passed to another state of existence. Forced by death to vacate his own material body, he will attach himself to a person still living on earth. People, usually those of weak characters, becoming so "possessed" by an earthbound spirit, are sometimes considered insane. A knowledge of psychic matters has, on many occasions, been the means of helping a so-called insane person to regain normality. To effect this, "rescue circles," as they are called, are held by experienced Spiritualists. The earthbound spirit is induced to release his hold on the victim's body and the obsessor is helped to free himself from his tormented condition.

Mr. Edward C. Randall had considerable success in this great work of freeing tortured souls.

The spirit of the unhappy earthbound butcher controlled Mr. Randall's medium. Asked what he experienced he exclaimed, "Eyes and noise. Nothing else. Everywhere eyes were looking at me. Over one half-million pairs of eyes. Think of it!"

Mr. Randall said, "They were the eyes of the animals you slaughtered, I suppose." "Yes," answered the earthbound spirit, "for thirty years I worked in the abbatoirs of the packing house."

He was asked whether he had looked into the eyes of every animal he killed and he replied, "Yes, and I still see them!"

The attorney said, "Do you know that every time you took the life of an animal and saw it looking at you, that look was recorded on your cosmic consciousness?"

Then he asked the "dead" butcher what was the cause of the noise of which he complained. The spirit replied, "The cries of the animals—sheep, steers, and the squeals of pigs—" Here the attorney broke in, "As the animals cried before you slaughtered them! That cry was also registered on your mind. When you left the body, there rolled before you the scroll of your life. You saw again all those eyes, and you heard the cries of lamentation of the animals that knew what was going to happen."

The tormented butcher exclaimed that his present environment was continually dripping with blood. He said that he would give anything to be relieved of his haunted condition.

Later, after he had succeeded in liberating the spirit from his miserable state, Mr. Randall told him, "You are free now, and can take up the new life and redeem yourself if you so desire."

When the "dead" butcher asked his benefactor whether animals, as well as humans, had continuity of life, he was assured that this was the case. "Where will I find them?" asked the spirit. "What can I do for them? That is what I want to know—especially the lambs."

The "dead" butcher was told by a spirit control, who was helping, that his atonement did not lie in the animal sphere, but in a different kind of service.

Before he left the body of the medium, the spirit, anxious already to begin a new life of service, said, "I would sooner take a chance in the hell of orthodoxy than the actual hell I have been through, that has been this day dispelled." Expressing the sorrow for all the thousands of men in the world who were doing what he had done, he said that he wished he could help them when they passed over.

"That may be your work," answered Mr. Randall as he bade him good-bye.

CHAPTER XX

MORAL IMPLICATIONS

L IKE most mediums, Mrs. Gladys Osborne Leonard is highly susceptible to vibrations which, for different reasons, charge the atmosphere of certain vicinities.

She told in "Psychic News" how, whenever she passed a particular corner in North London, a feeling of acute depression and apprehension stole over her.

Mrs. Leonard used to pass this spot whenever she walked to the library to change her books. It did not matter how happily she started out, the same feeling would overtake her at the identical place, and she found it difficult to overcome the condition until some time afterwards.

She began to wonder about the cause of this condition, but could find no personal explanation. Mrs. Leonard noted that the feeling would overtake her when she reached a high brick wall, with wide gates. The wall, which was of considerable length, surrounded a building which resembled a factory or storage place.

One day, Mrs. Leonard started to walk to the library at a different hour from her habitual one. When she reached the place where her depression usually occurred, she found that the high gates, generally closed when she passed, were wide open.

Through these gates she saw numbers of bullocks being led. "What is this place?" she asked a pedestrian. His reply was sufficient explanation for the feelings of apprehension and depression she had always experienced. The building, he told her, was a large slaughterhouse.

It is not surprising that such a sensitive as Mrs. Leonard should have been affected by the vibrations projected from a place where so many animals were slaughtered.

You may perhaps wonder what happens to the astral bodies of all these slaughtered creatures, often struck down in their prime in order to appease our appetites for flesh foods.

Mediums who have visited the animal spheres, either in trance or in sleep, have told us their experiences amongst such creatures.

Certain people have the psychic ability of astral travelling. As I have explained, we all possess an etheric or spirit counterpart to the physical body. The etheric body is attached to the physical one by a psychic rod. The Bible calls it the "silver cord." When this cord is completely severed, "death" takes place. The true self, manifesting through the etheric body, is removed to its real plane of existence.

When people, still on earth, temporarily leave their physical bodies, the etheric cord is still attached to the physical form. Were it not so, "death" would occur. That is the only difference between the two conditions of spirit travelling-the temporary, and the permanent.

Astral travelling happens to many of us during ordinary sleep, but we do not always remember our adventures.

Some people, however, are not only able to leave the physical body at will, but can remember what takes place during the separation. Mr. William Gerhardi, the well-known author, has written of his experiences of astral travelling.

Mrs. Leonard has told in her book, "My Life In Two Worlds," what she experienced when she left her physical body and visited the animal sphere. Here she saw the astral bodies of animals who had been slaughtered and projected suddenly into another plane of existence.

The medium writes, "One night I found myself leaving the physical body, but instead of the soaring upward motion, I had a heavy, weighted feeling, as if I were forced to travel in a horizontal position, and suddenly found myself in a narrow, dark street. I found I could just stand upright now, as if I were adjusting myself more easily to the atmosphere, but I did not want to put my feet on the ground as it was covered with mud and slime.

"Gloomy buildings, like stables, huddled against each other

so closely that they almost touched, leaving only sufficient room for one to walk between. Here and there I saw a wider opening, which appeared to lead into a kind of yard, into which the doors of some of the stables opened. I looked in and saw that the yard was crowded with animals-bullocks, pigs and sheep-dead, and yet alive. I *knew* they were dead, but I could also see that they were alive, too. They moved very slightly; many lay on the ground. I understood at once from their appearance that they had just been slaughtered.

"I pulled myself together with a tremendous effort. The place and everything in it was so horrible that I did indeed have to make an effort—a great one. I noticed that there was a great difference in the *substance* of this plane compared with that of the planes where I had seen ordinary discarnate human life… *This* dreadful place gave me the impression that it had but *temporary* existence. I will not go into more details of the place and the condition of the animals, but only tell you that it was indeed most dreadful and repulsive in every possible sense.

"I soon became aware that somebody was speaking to me, somebody whom I could not see, and who seemed to be a long way off. This person, who I afterwards found out was one of my spiritual Guides, told me that the place lay *between* the earth and etheric planes. Its misery was due to the tremendous slaughtering of animals for food that takes place daily; so much strong animal life is *suddenly* forced out of the actual physical condition into one that is very close indeed to earth, and yet is in no way part of the spiritual world…

"In the very air around me was a most definite feeling of terrible fear, suffering, and blind resentment that was even more tangible than the buildings and walls. My Guide told me that it was this awful *feeling* that was to be deplored, not only because it was an indication of the sufferings that these wretched animals had experienced, but because it affected the spiritual and mental atmosphere of the earth, and had a bad effect on human life and progress."

Mrs. Leonard described how this experience made her determined never to eat meat again. Before this experience she had not given thought to the fact that the flesh she ate had once walked and breathed, and felt discomfort and pain just as human beings experienced these conditions.

You may agree that the thought of the astral condition of slaughtered beasts is a distressing one. "But," you may ask, "what would happen if we did not kill all these animals? Would we not be overrun with cattle?"

You may also refer to the amount of destruction such animals as rabbits and foxes cause; you may argue that this destruction is at least kept in check by the killing of many of them.

Let us deal firstly with the question of cattle. If animals were not bred in order to supply our demand for flesh foods, the problem would solve itself.

There are thousands of healthy vegetarians who, with their easily acquired knowledge of what constitutes a balanced diet, prove that physical fitness does not depend upon the consumption of the bodies of animals. Most people who, for moral or for medical reasons, stopped eating meat, have improved considerably in health. Because of the rationing of meat in the Great War, numbers of people became enthusiastic converts to meatless diets. More recently, the revised rationing system has again swelled the vegetarian ranks.

If we stopped breeding cattle for purely selfish aims, their numbers would naturally decrease as the demand diminished. The patient cow, turned by humanity into a mechanical milking machine, would return to her own natural state. She would provide with milk only the ones nature intended her to succour—her own. offspring. Contrary to popular belief, cows' milk is not necessary for human health and infant upbringing.

The bull has suffered much from the hands of man. In the bullring be still provides entertainment at the expense of his life. In our own country, he suffers the indignity of being considered almost solely as a specialist in procreation. Perhaps, one day, this powerful animal will hold up his head again and we will learn to look into his eyes unashamed.

Although it is an unpleasant subject, you may feel bound to

ask, "What would happen if, because of our knowledge of the survival of all forms of life, we ceased to destroy verminous and filthy pests such as bugs, fleas and lice?"

There is an eventual solution to this problem. It is a simple one- an improved social order for men, women and children. Squalid and filthy dwellings must go, and pleasant, sanitary houses erected in their place. When this is effected—and much is being done to this end—vermin will be eliminated along with many other unjust discrepancies of life.

War, which brings so much horror in its wake, has also brought home to many of us the dreadful conditions under which some people have to live. The evacuation of children, infested with vermin, has caused much trouble in the homes they have entered.

The habits of some of the evacuated mothers revolted those who have never known the despair of squalor. It is almost impossible to keep clean under some conditions, and degeneration of decent sanitary habits sometimes follows.

Although the evacuated poor shocked many of us, they made us realise that slum dwellings, and the need for living in them, must be wiped out. Human beings will learn that life is more attractive in clean surroundings than in sordid conditions. There are, I know, certain people so imbibed in squalor they do not mind it. But their generation will pass.

What of such insect pests as mosquitoes which, as most people know, are carriers of malaria?

Well, cleansing of their breeding-places is now scientifically carried out. It will help eventually to exterminate these disease transmitters. Much success in this direction has already been achieved.

You may perhaps speak of the possibility of being overrun by certain species of wild creatures if we did not destroy them either for "sport" or in a businesslike way.

The truth is that, because we kill so many species of animals, we become infested with too many of another kind. The superfluity of these unwanted creatures is brought about, to a great extent, by upsetting the balance of nature's requirements. When we interfere too deeply, we must pay the price.

When animals have ceased to serve their useful purpose the species die out. The dodo is as dead as—the dodo! The enormous prehistoric creatures have become extinct, as others have evolved and developed.

Nature, left to herself, has her own methods of dealing with these problems.

The knowledge that animals survive "death" brings moral obligations and a sense of responsibility to the human who is aware of this fact. He may have gained the knowledge through logical reasoning, psychic evidence, or by inner conviction alone. He will realise that in addition to the higher animals who survive as individual personalities, even the most lowly of living creatures attain some degree of continuity of existence.

Because he knows that animals survive "death" a person may ask himself whether he is justified in continuing to eat the flesh of a creature bred and slaughtered to satisfy his appetite. If, knowing that there are plenty of appetising alternatives to flesh foods, he finds the desire for meat irresistible, that is a matter for the individual's own conscience.

If, after honest consideration, those believing in the survival of animals can continue to kill for sport-that, too, is their own affair. We are our own judges of right and wrong.

A woman may question her own responsibility in wearing furs, the skins of animals caught and often tortured before she can adorn herself.

Some of us, indeed, may even question, in the light of our knowledge, whether we are justified in killing obnoxious pests.

Well, the world is still far from perfect. Until a better one is evolved by the lives we lead, we must strike a temporary balance, never losing sight of the vision ahead.

If certain animals and pests have, at our present stage of evolution, to be destroyed, they should be exterminated as painlessly as possible.

Those who still find the eating of flesh irresistible should at least make sure that the living creature was not subjected to cruelty before or during slaughter.

Prior to reaching your table, such game as pheasant may have been wounded by the gun of a clumsy "sportsman" and lingered in pain before it breathed its last.

A capon is a castrated chicken. Its reproductive glands have been torn from its body in order to improve the quality of the flesh. This operation is carried out without the aid of anaesthetics. Because it is not always done by practised hands, it is often clumsily performed.

The well known table delicacy, foie gras, is obtained from the diseased livers of forceably over-fed geese. The live birds are confined in quarters too cramped to allow them to move freely. Their crops are over-filled with food by means of a cramming machine.

As a result of this cruel treatment, the birds' livers become diseased. The geese are then killed, and foie gras is prepared from their enlarged livers.

Unfortunately, cramming of poultry is now extensively practised in this island, although it is forbidden by law in certain other countries.

The Jewish method of slaughtering animals is a cruel one. It has led many a humane orthodox Jew who would not break away from the tenets of his faith to refrain from eating meat altogether. You may be a woman who cannot resist the appeal of furs. There are some animals whose manner of trapping would appal you if you knew how it was done. Therefore, find out which furs are obtained by particularly cruel devices. Such organisations as the Animal Defence Society will advise you.

Incidentally, "synthetic" furs are manufactured these days. They are made from materials which have the appearance of the real skins. Most of the stores sell them nowadays. The Duchess of Hamilton wore imitation ermine on her robes at the Coronation of King George VI.

But—if you want to continue to wear real furs—I advise you never to read "Pilgrims Of The Wild" by Grey Owl!

CHAPTER XXI

THE LION AND THE LAMB

YOU will recall that Silver Birch told us that nature's balance altered in accordance with the evolution of the humans who dwell in this world, and that the further humanity advanced the less of nature's darkness would there be.

He said that when mankind had reached the stage where love and kindness were accepted by all, there would be no ferocity amongst the beasts—the lion would lie down with the lamb!

I do not consider this to be at all inconceivable or beyond the realms of probability or possibility. I believe that "Nature red in tooth and claw" will, at some time or another, become transformed into a tranquililty of existence between all living creatures—humanity included. It may be a dream at present. But often in life's history dreams have materialised into reality. We ourselves can hasten their realisation by living in unity, wherever and whenever possible, with natural laws.

Symbiosis—successful partnership between living organisms—already operates amongst certain plants, animals, birds and insects.

Although, at the present time, symbiosis does not function in every phase of nature, H. Reinheimer in his book "Symbiosis" declares that *only* the animals and plants that co-operate for the common good may attain permanent survival in evolution.

He says, "My thesis with regard to evolution is that everything normal and sound in organic evolution is due to biologically righteous, *i.e.* essentially co-operative behaviour; whilst everything abnormal and pathological is due to unrighteous, *i.e.* fundamentally predatory behaviour. Although predatory species may apparently, and for a time, live quite well, yet their temporary success is at the expense of permanent survival."

This author points out that, contrary to popular conception, the more predaceous the animal, the more diseased its organism. He says, "We have as yet to rid our minds of a good deal of prejudice even regarding our terrestial carnivora. Some may think of the lion as a 'king of animals,' but in reality he is a 'sick man' and has little chance of survival with the advance of 'organic civilisation.' He stands for 'might is right,' and, therefore, he has to go."

When symbiosis is adequately expressed throughout the realms of nature, animals will no longer prey upon each other, and man will live in harmony and peace with his neighbour, enjoying the bounty that the Creator has provided for all who dwell in His kingdom.

A similar idea of symbiotic living was expressed by Silver Birch in answer to some of the questions put to him.

At every stage of life we have the vanguards as well as the retrogrades. Even in the imperfect world of today, we sometimes get the strange anomaly of animals, who are usually natural enemies, living in harmony with each other.

I remember seeing a nature film called "Sequoia." This film, presented by Metro-Goldwyn-Mayer Company, depicted the friendship of a deer and a puma.

The director of this artistic presentation says that these two hereditary enemies were raised together from infancy and they learned naturally to be friends. When they were fully grown, they were turned loose into the Giant Redwood Forest of Sequoia National Park. Here they were filmed together amongst their own natural surroundings. No camera tricks were used in making this pictorial record of the unusual friendship which existed between two born enemies.

The ferret is well known for its lust for blood. Yet the story of a friendship between two ferrets and a kitten is told in "Animal Pictorial."

The owner writes, "Happening to have two three-quarter grown white ferrets and a half-grown kitten at the same time, it occurred to me to see if such a friendship could be established. All three were accordingly given their morning milk in a common bowl, and a careful watch kept, the ferrets being removed immediately either showed signs of hostility. After about a week it was found possible to dispense with the mollifying influence of the milk. At first the kitten was intensely nervous, but curiosity overcame this, and the love of play common to all young animals broke down the barriers of antagonistic species.

"When the three grew up, the affection remained," concludes the writer.

So that humans may indulge their taste for "sport," hounds are encouraged to hunt and harry the fox.

But Mrs. George Machin, of Lincolnshire, who has now passed on, brought up fox cubs and hounds in perfect happiness and harmony. Her daughter tells me that, when a vixen was caught in a trap, she had to be destroyed. To save her two cubs from starvation, they were taken to Mrs. Machin's home at Ussleby Hall. They were fed from a baby's bottle, and when Charlie and Billy, as they were called, grew out of the baby stage, they were introduced to Helpful and Headful, two hound puppies from the Brocklesby Kennels.

The four young animals at once became playmates and used to feed together from the same dish. "It was really most delightful to see the quartet romping together," says Miss Machin. "The cubs were very long in the leg and their movements were so quick and agile that they had a great advantage over the clumsy, fat puppies."

When the time came for the two hounds to leave for other kennels, the cubs were so disconsolate that the family had to introduce them to another dog, this time a young terrier, who soon struck up a great friendship with the foxes.

Another unusual friendship was that of a seven-year-old Manx cat and a young robin. "The Standard," a Montreal newspaper, told how this friendship came about.

A Manx cat belonging to Mrs. Clinton W. Baker brought her an injured robin held gently in its mouth. The young bird had apparently fallen from its nest. It was taken into the house and soon recovered sufficiently to hop about the room. From that time, the cat assumed guardianship over the robin and the two became great friends. When the bird was able to fly, it was taken out of doors and given its freedom. But it would never venture far away from the house of its friend the cat.

At meal-times, the robin would call to be let into the house. After it had been fed, it would snuggle up with the cat for a nap. The bird showed fear of strangers and other cats, but was always happy and at peace with the one who had brought it to safety when it was injured.

The following story appeared in the "Daily Mirror" "A cat, a dog and a rabbit were 'mourners' at a solemnly conducted funeral at Prestwood, High Wycombe, of Mike, a ten-year-old tabby, cat. Mike was known as everybody's friend because of the strange attachments he made... His closest friend had been a big thrush. Every day for months the thrush would perch himself on Mike's back and tickle his ears with his beak. Mike, in return, would wash the thrush's back. Then, one day, the thrush vanished. Mike became depressed. He was killed under a bus just outside his house a week after his friend's disappearance."

Tommy, a Persian cat, allowed himself to be photographed for the Toronto "Daily Star" with a small white mouse for whom the cat had taken a strong liking. The pair would play together as though it was the ordinary thing to do. When the newspaper photographer visited the cat's home, Tommy gathered the mouse into his paws and posed for his picture quite happily!

CHAPTER XXII

A GIFT FROM BEYOND

BY means of spirit power, material objects are sometimes carried from one place to another.

These apports, as they are called, are often brought to a seance room by a spirit guide or control and presented to sitters.

All sorts of objects have been received in this way. Usually, they have little material value, but their method of presentation naturally makes them gifts of great value to the recipient.

How these material objects are transported from one place to another by supernormal methods is not exactly known. It seems that the physical object is reduced to its non-material basis during transportation, and then reassembled in its original form in the séance room.

The spirit guides always emphasise that these gifts are not stolen. They are sometimes unwanted objects. Sometimes, they are articles that have been buried in the earth. Once it was explained by a guide that the apports he had brought that night—some semiprecious stones—had been carried from a lost property office on the Continent where they had been "written off" as surplus and valueless. Others have been recovered by spirit power from sunken vessels.

I have received several such apports from spirit people. I prize these gifts immensely.

Some time ago, during a séance held by Mrs. Louisa Bolt, I was given a beautifully coloured glass miniature of a dog's head. It probably once formed part of a locket. Because of the clever way the head has been carved in the glass, it gives a particularly life-like impression. I was naturally delighted with the gift. "How very appropriate!" said some of my friends. "You probably received it because you are so fond of animals."

I now think there might have been even a little more significance attached to the gift than the suggested one.

When I heard about the "death" of my friends' dog and was considering the writing of this book, I chanced to look at the miniature again. Something I had never before noticed aroused my attention. I saw that the dog's face was so intelligent that it had an almost human expression. The eyes seemed to speak. "Tell them about me," they implored. "Tell them about all of us. Tell them we are not *really* dead!"

I wonder if that is why I received the apport.

CHAPTER XXIII

NO MORE TEARS

IN the light of knowledge that animals survive "death" an owner of a beloved pet may ask, "Should I have had him `put to sleep'?"

This is a matter for the individual to decide. There are many circumstances where it may be considered the kindest thing to have done. But make sure that the method to be used for ending your animal's earthly life is in keeping with humanitarian principles. Some methods of "humane" killing are humane in name only. The stricken pet should be assisted into the next world by gentle, but experienced professional hands.

There is no doubt that your pet, on regaining consciousness in another sphere, will receive immediate care and loving attention from those whose work is to help the newly awakened animals.

Mrs. Florence Kingstone, the medium who has brought so much comfort to those whose pets have passed on, told me how, in sleep state, she once visited the animal plane. There she saw the astral bodies of a number of cats and dogs who were just recovering from the effects of being "put to sleep."

Some of these animals were still sound asleep, others were just rousing themselves, whilst some, apparently, had just awakened into full consciousness. Possibly because they were all bathed in a beautiful effect of sunlight, they all appeared to be of the same pale golden hue. Yet, Mrs. Kingstone could clearly see that the coat of each animal had its own individual and distinct marking.

The whole atmosphere was one of light and restfulness.

Do not mourn the loss of your pets more than you can help. It will distress them when they come to see you. Animals have simple, unquestioning minds; they are rather like children in their natural acceptance of the love you bear them. They will not understand your grief because they reason that, not only are they alive and well, but are by your side. It will distress them to see your tears, for they cannot understand your reasons for shedding then.

Remember, the pet you have lost for a while will awaken to perfect health, with all ills vanished. One of the first things he will do will be to return to prove to you what a fine fellow he has become again. Help him to realise you know he is present by giving him a word or two of encouragement. Speak to him in the old accustomed way he knows so well. He will often visit you. Let him know that a welcome still awaits him.

You may not have the psychic power to see the dog who has returned, so full of health and vigour. You may not be able; to feel the presence of the cat who, with regained well-being, will rub her sleek, complacent form against the human who always lavished such loving care upon' her. You may not hear the song of the pet bird whose notes of gladness have taken on an added sweetness. You may not be fortunate enough to see your animals every time they visit you.

Nevertheless, be happy in the knowledge that, if the tie of love still binds, your "dead" pets will be there to greet you when the time comes for you to rejoin them.

And, even at the risk of being thought lacking in delicacy and understanding, I give the following advice to you whose. animal may recently have passed on. As soon as it is practicable, get another one! You need not necessarily get the same breed, or even the same species as the one who has temporarily left you. But, believe me, this act will help you enormously, even though the new pet may never take the place in your heart of the former one.

When my first cat "died" I took the same advice, which I have never regretted. My second cat "Paddy—the next best thing"— as I called him, proved a blessed consolation.

There are other reasons, too, why you should, get another animal. There are so many who need your love and care—a surplus kitten about to be destroyed, a homeless dog, a lost cat.

Maybe, in the shop that sells dogs, there is a pathetic little fellow looking out appealingly from his confined space in the window. He is waiting for someone on whom he can bestow a life of loyalty and devotion. A soul, full of love, shines from the eyes that search the faces of the passers-by so eagerly.

He is probably looking for you!